TRUE STORIES
The Narrative Project
Volume III

EDITED BY

Cami Ostman
Rebecca Mabanglo-Mayor
Anneliese Kamola
Wendy Welch
Nancy Canyon
Colleen Haggerty

TRUE STORIES
The Narrative Project
Volume III

EDITED BY

Cami Ostman, Rebecca Mabanglo-Mayor,
Anneliese Kamola, Wendy Welch,
Nancy Canyon, Colleen Haggerty

Sidekick Press
Bellingham, Washington

Publisher's Note: Portions of this work are memoir. Names, characters, places, and incidents are products of the authors' recollection. Some names of individuals have been changed. Locales and public names are sometimes used for atmospheric purposes. Any resemblance to actual people, living or dead, or to businesses, companies, events, institutions, or locales is completely coincidental. Fictional pieces in this anthology reflect the imagination of the authors. Each individual author is responsible for the content of their work.

Sidekick Press
2950 Newmarket Street
Suite 101-329
Bellingham, Washington 98226
www.sidekickpress.com

True Stories—The Narrative Project, Volume III
ISBN 978-1-7344945-2-5
LCCN 2018961451

Cover Design: Spoken Designs www.spokendesigns.com

Dedication

For Jessica H. Stone, who brought our stories to life for two volumes and has graduated to working on her own books. We bless you on your journey, Story Warrior!

INTRODUCTION

Dear Reader,

In your hand you hold a true collaboration. I'm fond of telling our writers in The Narrative Project that "writers don't let writers write alone." I say this because I know, without reservation, that every piece of writing I've ever finished and put out into the world came to completion because I had people supporting me and holding me accountable for the work.

The authors represented in this third volume of True Stories are not only friends and fans of one another, but they are each other's critique partners, beta readers, and accountability allies. Each of the pieces you will read in these pages represents a portion of a larger work. Writing a book is a practice as much as it is a thing you do. You have to put time on your calendar to show up to the story. Then you've got to get feedback on what you've written, revise it, and send it back for more feedback. You've got to conceptualize and re-conceptualize the big picture. And you've got to make sure you balance the story you're telling with the themes you're exploring. This means you need witnesses to your work along the way and lots of support for the inevitable moments when the journey feels daunting. Every piece in this book is such a joint effort.

As you enjoy and are touched by what The Narrative Project community has wrought here, may you think of your own stories—those truths crying out to be told. May you be encouraged to put pen to paper or fingers to the keyboard and flesh out the first draft of something that, with the right support, can become a complete work you can one day hold in your hand and give to your loved ones as a gift.

Stories are the units of meaning-making, dear friends. We tell and read and write them because they make our lives come into focus and help us construct our understanding of reality together.

With this volume...welcome to our narrative community.

Cami Ostman, Your Chief Story Warrior

CONTENTS

Arlington by August Cabrera 1

A Terrible Storm by Nancy Canyon 11

Dames with Comics by Al Clover 23

Losing Control by Lisa Dailey 35

Unbearably Beautiful by Seán Dwyer.................................. 49

1941, London by Colleen Haggerty 61

The Kind of People Who Leave Dirt on the Floor
    by Alyson Indrunas.. 73

Something to Remember Me By
    by Anneliese Kamola 81

Adirondack Chairs by Christina Kemp 93

Never Heard by Rebecca Mabanglo-Mayor 101

Resilience by Judith Mayotte 111

Violence by G. Annie Ormsby.. 123

Quest of the Buckwheaters by Aaron C Palmer................. 137

All about Tristan by Kathy Wagner 151

Desert Daughter by M. F. Webb 163

Appalachian Yankees by Wendy Welch............................ 175

Scars by Diane Wood... 181

Arlington
by August Cabrera

June is always too hot in DC, so I had asked for the ceremony to be held as early as possible. I didn't want to be crowded, on display, and overheated. And besides, the boys didn't do well when they were too warm. It seemed like the prudent thing to do to have the service before the busloads of tourists arrived, and the cemetery was willing to agree to my request. Maybe it was because they knew cars would be lined three-deep on the street prior to the procession and they wanted this particularly high-profile funeral out of the way. Maybe the organizers—friends of mine—had made a plea since there were so many kids involved. Maybe the status of the dead soldier in question lent some weight to their decision. No matter the reason, the event started first thing in the morning, but it was already getting uncomfortably sticky by the time the dozens and dozens of cars began their slow drive through the roads of Arlington National Cemetery.

Arlington is beautiful. Unnaturally healthy grass with rows upon rows upon rows of identical tombstones, all lined up in a precise manner. If you stand at the right angle it appears as though the markers—each etched with the name, rank, birth and death dates, and a short epitaph—reach on into infinity. It is an optical illusion, of course, much like when you stand between two mirrors and your reflection seems to stretch back into forever. The clear blue sky, the bright green grass, the stark white stones, all balanced against a perfectly selected, demure, sleeveless, Calvin Klein black dress.

When I arrived—plenty early I thought to wrestle with what I had assumed would be a manageable crowd—I was overwhelmed by the size of the group that had already gathered. A dark feeling floated among those who felt led to come to pay their final respects, but there were also hellos and hugs shared between people who had traveled from all over the country. Some hadn't seen each other in months, others in years. Friends intermingled with family who introduced themselves to the obvious Army connections dressed in full dress uniforms. At one point I saw my boys, only six and seven at the time, find their older half-brother and sister, Corbin and Gillian, and run to them for hugs. I knew my boys were okay at the moment, so I allowed myself time to be the proper military widow and gave a hundred hugs to those I knew and what felt like that many awkward handshakes to those in formal attire.

We were still an hour out from the beginning of the ceremony and I had yet to meet the on-site coordinator. She would run the show, clipboard in one hand, radio in the other. During an interlude in the pre-event chaos, my escorting General offered a moment of quiet in the Women in Military Service for America Memorial building. There was a restroom and a bit of peace away from the crowd that felt like it would swallow me up at any moment. He walked me into the building and patiently waited while I checked my hair and makeup one last time in the bathroom mirror. There was a photographer from *The Washington Post* with the group and I knew pictures of this would accompany the article that was due to be published later that year.

Jim Scheeler, a *Post* reporter, would be the one writing about Dave. He had met him a few years earlier when he had been working on a piece about mental health support in the military. Dave, as a PhD social worker in the Army, made for a great interview. Dave could talk to anyone about anything, especially if he was passionate about the subject and he was definitely passionate about military behavioral health. When Dave was killed in October, a mutual friend reached out to Jim to share the news. A few months later he contacted me to ask if he could do a story on Dave for the Veteran's Day issue of *The Washington Post Magazine*. I agreed. I wanted everyone to know about Dave. I had already done TV and newspaper interviews in Houston, and I wanted the whole world to know what an amazing man my husband had been and that he died doing what he loved—helping soldiers. Saying yes to the *Post* article was an easy decision.

Jim had come out a few days before the ceremony for interviews and candid shots for the article. He and his photographer spent a few hours with me at the house asking lots of questions and asking to see pictures and notes Dave had left me.

Since I'd known both Jim and the photographer would be at Arlington, I knew I needed to look the part. I spent weeks trying to find the perfect dress: flattering in pictures, but not sexy at all. I tried on a dozen pairs of shoes looking for the ones that were high enough to match the dress style, but comfortable enough to wear all day. I shopped for the perfect pair of sunglasses that did not overpower my small face, but still gave me a bit of privacy under the slightly oversized lenses. I wore my Lancôme mascara, which I joked was "widow tested and widow approved" for its magical ability to stay on even in the most extreme emotional circumstances. My only compromise was my hairstyle. When I went to get my hair cut before Arlington I asked my hairdresser what would be the most appropriate cut for a public appearance with a lot of photos. His suggestion was a short bob, but I was in the process of trying to grow out my curls so I left my hair longer and thought to myself, *I guess they will have to handle a little bit of sexy.*

Everything but my hair was chosen for appearances that day. I knew I had a part to play and I was a willing participant in making it look as perfect as possible. Was this shallow? Yes. Absolutely. But my clothes and my curls gave me something to control in the midst of the formulaic and very tightly-scripted ceremony.

I looked at my reflection in the mirror one last time, breathed in what felt like my last private breath of the day, and walked back out into the memorial building to the waiting General. He took my arm and we walked back outside, finding the coordinator who explained how it would all play out. I would be in the lead car and we would all drive in a procession to the point where our group met with the Caisson Platoon. Dave's ashes would be passed from the car to the solider in charge of transferring him into the small door in the side of the flag-draped coffin. The coffin would then be pulled behind the horses to Section 60, where the ceremony would take place. I was told I could choose to walk behind the Caisson Platoon holding onto the arm of the General or get back in the car and be driven the few blocks to Section 60. Once everyone arrived at the burial site, the formal proceedings would begin. I was strongly urged by the Army organizers to get back in the car after the transfer because if I chose to walk, it would force all the other mourners to walk as well.

I had planned on following my instructions, I really had.

At exactly the agreed upon moment, the procession began. I sat in the backseat of the car—though I don't remember whose car it actually was or even who was driving for that matter—and rode to the place where we met up with the waiting Caisson Platoon. I had given Dave's urn to someone else the day before because they were worried I would forget to bring his ashes the next morning. I'm not sure who "they" were and I don't have any idea how I could forget my husband's urn, but it really didn't matter to me at that point as I had made my peace with his remains months earlier.

I got out of the car to witness the transfer, watching as his ashes were carefully inserted into the coffin, which was used often enough there was a small worn patch where the door was closed to securely hold the Army-issued urn. My job was to simply get back in the car and ride the rest of the way to his burial site. But I couldn't do it. Riding in that car to Section 60 somehow seemed so disrespectful. So, I took the General's waiting arm and we began the slow walk behind the horses with what felt like two hundred people behind me. My boys walked on one side of me, the General on the other. My stepkids were right there too at the front of the parade, walking side by side with their mother, just as it should be.

And then the sound started.

Swoosh. Click. *Swoosh.* Click. *Swoosh.* Click.

Those damn shoes.

I was doing my level best to channel my inner-Jackie O for this dog and pony show, and I somehow ended up with a pair of shoes that did this strange swooshy-squeaky sound with every step of my right foot. Really, what would the General think? Who else could hear my *faux pas*? I was embarrassed, ashamed, feeling like a fraud. I was supposed to hold it together—that was my one and only job, hold it all together—and I messed the entire thing up with these stupid black leather, peep-toed Clarks heels. Every step behind the Platoon. Every step closer to Section 60. Every step toward the chairs set up in respectful rows on the perfectly-manicured grass. Every step to the final moment I would be able to see what was left of Dave in his tasteful, mahogany urn. Every step my stupid shoes reminded me of what a failure I was at this whole widow thing.

The General was walking next to me, white gloves to hold my arm, close enough to hear my shoes. I looked at my small boys walking so bravely next to me, in their matching black button-down shirts and khakis, with the little one wearing one of his daddy's Mickey Mouse ties, and I realized they needed me more than I needed to be held up by yet another man wearing dress blues.

I let go of the General, quietly telling him thank you, and grabbed my boys' hands in mine. I wondered, as I reached for them, what the General would think of yet another *faux pas*. I was so busy worrying about all the trouble I was going to get into by letting go of my official escort, listening to my shoes, and hoping my makeup wasn't running from the humidity, that I forgot what I was doing.

I didn't smell the freshly cut grass. I didn't feel the small boy hands in mine. I didn't hear the sound of Dave's wedding ring worn on a chain around my neck as it made a dull thud against my chest with each step.

I just worried about my shoes.

We wound our way to the site set up for the service. There were two lines of tasteful white chairs and everyone knew their seat assignments. Only twelve people were seated, and there was bit of a fuss when someone not on the list sat down without knowing the backstory negotiations about the arrangements. Just like at the formal, military funeral in Houston back in November, I sat between Dave's dad and my boys. My step-kids and their mom made up the rest of the front row. The rest of the chairs were taken up by carefully-selected mourners, though I had left that decision mostly up to the organizers of the whole thing. I had played my one card during the planning by insisting my step-kids got to sit next to their mom, even if it looked strange to have the ex-wife in the pictures. Her kids needed her, and so I forced the issue.

The ceremony started.

There were words. None of which I remember.

Apparently, a folded flag was handed to me on behalf of a Grateful Nation.

A bugler must have played "Taps" at a respectful distance.

And maybe a twenty-one-gun salute, but I'm not sure. I remember being startled by something that morning, but the actual memory is vague at best.

And then it was over.

People milled around, unsure what to do next. Did they make small talk? Should they approach me? Was it okay to make the trek back to their cars and get on with their lives? It was all very awkward. Finally, I worked up my strength to request a moment alone with Dave. Asking for what I wanted felt out of step with the expectations in front of me, some implicit, some explicit. I knew I wasn't supposed to break down having a conversation with Dave's ashes; that could look bad in pictures. I also knew I walked a fine line between grieving widow and trophy widow and I wasn't very happy with the tension between those two roles this hot June morning.

The uniforms in charge graciously asked people to clear the space around the small, short table that held the urn. There are not a lot of concrete memories from that day, but I very clearly remember kneeling at the green, cloth-covered table, placing one hand on each side of the remarkably small wooden box, lowering my head, and sobbing. Between ragged breaths I told Dave how much I missed him. How much the kids missed him. And then I told him over and over again how sorry I was. I was sorry I had agreed he could go to Afghanistan. Now he was dead and it was my fault.

Even though I was wearing the right mascara and had the right sunglasses on, it wouldn't stop everyone from seeing my carefully-applied eye makeup running down my cheeks. This was not the time to show any actual emotion, my job was to hold it together in public, just as I had for the eight months leading up to his interment. If I could have pulled that off, I would have been a success, though at this point, I wasn't sure what that even meant beyond a sense of approval I hoped to gain. From someone. Somewhere. At some point.

I'm not sure how long I was there, though it was long enough for the *Post* photographer to snap a picture of me in that position: head dropped, long reddish curls covering my face, back curved in anguish, a backdrop of rows upon rows of military-precise, white headstones leading to the horizon filled with thousands of other dead soldiers. That picture was the cover of

The Washington Post Magazine in November; I was not told it would be used in the piece, let alone as the cover.

I never meant to be a news item. I was just a broken woman trying to keep a tenuous hold on my world while properly honoring the memory of my husband, the hero, by getting it all right. Just like I failed him when I agreed to his voluntary deployment to Afghanistan, I failed him again in Arlington when my very human grief overshadowed my clearly defined role as a properly-managed military widow. Even if just for a moment. Just one click of the camera. My failure was obvious to anyone watching.

A Terrible Storm
by Nancy Canyon

Silence thrums on and on at six thousand feet. It's like the sky
and trees and everything else give off a sound. The silence can
be pretty dang loud, lonely even, and at the same time, completely quiet. The telephone never rings, or rarely even works.
Once it was used to report wildfires. Arizona, our boss, said,
"If you want to call home, you can." But, like I said, the
phone barely works.

Some folks don't like telephones. My brother for one. I
can never get him to call me. And when I call Dad, I always
feel like I must be polite first. I should say, "Hi, how are you?
How's your new wife?" before I say, "Can I borrow the
truck?" or "Could you loan me money to buy a new camera?"
or whatever I think I need, like money to pay medical bills.
So, I put off calling. Mostly, I write letters these days.

But every child needs a father's help when leaving the
nest. So here I am on the lookout tower looking at a ringing
telephone, imagining it's Dad calling. I feel a little storm
brewing in my chest. "What, already?" I say, staring down the

receiver without picking up. This is how it is when you're dull from isolation and worn out from the blasted heat.

My husband, Jack, steps inside from the catwalk. "Answer, for fuck's sake."

I shrug. "No one's calling back, since we didn't call anyone."

He knows that the line is usually broken. We've seen how it's strung through the forest, draped over tree limbs all the way from the tower to the town at the farmer's place. Well, it's not actually a town, just a junction of two roads where the farmer has lived forever.

"Maybe Mom is sick," I say. "Or something has happened to my sister. She's basically unsupervised since the divorce, you know." With that thought, I jump up to grab the receiver. "Hello? Hello?" Nothing.

"Shit, static's causing the phone to ring." Jack turns to the horizon, squinting hard. "A storm's building!"

"Doesn't look like a storm to me," I say, still holding the receiver in my hand. I put it to my ear and listen to the dial tone buzzing on and on.

"I've heard that electricity can come through a line. Sky's thickening. This could be bad, Nance."

I nod, staying focused on the big black thing, much like a pay phone, only we can dial it without adding coins. When we first arrived, Arizona said, "When you call out, call collect. If the phone works, that is."

Jack is a bundle of over-firing nerves, no different than when we married two years ago. We could use some connection with the outside world right about now. He's pulling at his mustache, standing straight and expectant as he stares at the receiver I'm holding. He reaches out his hand and waggles his fingers at me. Our cat, Jude, wanders between us as if she couldn't care less about static on the phone.

I hand the phone over, knowing he'll hear the same dial tone that I hear, since it's "electricity" calling. I think of that sparky character the electric company uses in its advertisements: a lightning bolt cartoon who's always in a hurry. We are definitely not in a hurry. We are watchers of the sky and hills, shy and vulnerable escapists wishing there was something tangible between the molecules that we could grab hold of. I wish we could clutch those molecules tight to our chests so we don't feel so much pain. Such fierce loneliness.

But these are my words, not Jack's. Jack never admits to feeling pain, but God, his mother just died. Man, he feels heavy to me right now.

His mother's massive hemorrhage was caused by a bit of tissue growing in her heart, breaking off, and traveling to her brain. The doctors theorized that the nub was from a bout of rheumatic fever she suffered as a child. My brother had rheumatic fever as a child. I wonder if he has a nodule in his heart.

I always say I had nothing happen to me growing up: no broken bones, no mumps, and no chicken pox. But I did have the week-long measles, though I barely felt sick. And, I did have other things to deal with, like Dad coming to my bedroom every chance he got. I so wish I'd known he wasn't my real father back then, just a stepdad abusing his adopted daughter. If I had known that, it could have made a world of difference. I think it would have, anyway.

Here I am now, standing by the phone, watching Jack's hazel eyes turn cartoonlike, a silly character about to run off a cliff.

"Who would call?" Jack says. "Your dad? My dad?"

I shrug. I have a hard time calling Jack's father "Dad," though Squeak says I should. "I'm your dad too, now that you're married."

My dad didn't want me to marry Jack, and because I went against his wishes, he's been giving me the cold shoulder ever since. Squeak said to me once when I was crying because Dad wasn't speaking to me, "You have me. I'm here for you. You can't get rid of me."

I sigh, remove the receiver from Jack's hand and hang it up. "It's static, like you said. And look, the horizon's as thick as a winter blanket."

During a lightning storm, it is best to sit in the green chair with the glass insulators cupping each of the legs. Either there or on the bed—just stay out from between two metal objects, such as the Osborne Firefinder and the gas stove. Lightning could arc between two metal objects and fry you like chicken.

My mother says lightning will come through a broken windowpane. She grew up in the East with frequent thunderstorms roaring through her town. Now, whenever a storm's brewing, she runs around the house, closing up all the windows. When the wind comes up, she's beside herself with nerves. I think she passed that behavior onto me, because when the wind blows, I bite my fingernails with a vengeance. Right now, however, I'm feeling pretty excited by the storm I see building over Camas Prairie—huge cumulonimbus blooming like giant mushroom clouds.

Once, when I was a kid, the wind came up while we were picnicking in Comstock Park. Mom immediately headed for the car. Cars are supposed to be safe, with rubber tires insulating passengers from lightning. I followed, climbing into the backseat. She sat in the front, chain smoking, a white haze curling around her head and throughout the car.

I said, "You should stop smoking."

She said, "Mind your own business."

"It is my business. You could die."

She got grouchy as hell after that and wouldn't talk to me. Outside, the clouds blackened and thunder rumbled around the neighborhood. We waited for Dad, and my brother and sister to return from a friend's house, so we could go home. Soon rain started falling and Mom rolled up the windows. The car filled with smoke and humidity, and I held my breath, rolling my window down a bit to gulp fresh air. She snapped at me to close it. *Lightning, you know—*

That was after we'd eaten all the chicken and potato salad together as a family and Dad remembered his business friend lived nearby. We packed up the picnic in the trunk of the car and walked across the street to pay him, his wife, and kid a visit. Right away, his daughter and I hit it off. We ran around the house, looking at all their neat stuff. The girl'd just baked two loaves of bread with her mother and she gave me one. When we were getting ready to leave, I stood there holding a loaf of still-warm bread in my hands.

Dad said, "What do you think you're doing?"

"She gave it to me," I said.

"Give it back," he said, and got that mean look on his face, the one that drills clear through a person, scaring them to death.

I don't remember why Mom and I ended up in the car that day without my brother and sister, but there I was, getting the cold treatment from the back of my mother's head as the storm blackened the sky west of town. While growing up, there was always a storm brewing in our family, one that didn't require closing up windows.

Now, cumulonimbus bloom into huge anvils over the prairie. Lightning flashes from cloud to cloud and occasionally, cloud to ground. We wander around the tower, feeling uneasy, as if we're waiting for the bad thing to happen. We don't know whether to eat or read or twiddle our thumbs while we wait for the tempest to arrive. I pace the room, my gaze falling upon a cracked windowpane. I point it out to Jack. "Lightning could come through that crack. Better call Arizona on the two-way radio and tell him."

"Go ahead!"

"I feel stupid calling and complaining about a cracked pane when the summer's nearly half over." I imagine pressing the handset button and saying nothing, or mumbling something incoherent like I did in high school English class one day. I was so happy to be called upon by Mr. Finner, but then nothing but gibberish came out of my mouth. I was terribly embarrassed. "Will you call?" I say. "The lightning could come inside and kill us."

He faces the pane and the prairie beyond, pulling at his mustache, sticking hairs in his mouth and chewing. A large lightning bolt brightens the sky over Grangeville.

"Please?"

Finally, he picks up the radio handset and calls the district. Arizona laughs when he learns of the problem. "Sit on the bed," he says, "away from the broken pane."

"That's just it," Jack says. "The window is next to the bed."

"When we pick up trash next, we'll fix it. In the meantime, tape it up. Anything else?"

"Nope," Jack says, looking sheepish.

"Then enjoy the storm. Over and out."

Hissing, he hangs up the receiver. Clouds blot out the sky, bringing dusk early. The prairie disappears as the storm heads toward us. Multiple bolts, jagged and bright, sear the view. One after another, a flurry of strikes; too many to count and certainly too many to record in the strike log. I pull the log out from beneath a stack of papers anyway. I carry it with me to the bed, feeling as if I'm walking to the gallows.

Jack climbs onto the bed next to me and leans close. "It'll be all right, Nancerella."

"I know," I say, "it's just that it's moving so fast. We've never seen anything...."

I know that the rate the storm's building and the frequency of the bolts point to the worst storm we've had since we arrived two months ago. A transformer blows on the prairie; an explosion of bright sparking light illuminating the darkness. Then another transformer. Then, what appears to be a ball of lightning lifts off the ground high into the air, hovering there momentarily, then settling back again. "Did you see that?"

"Yep, ball lightning. It's a natural phenomenon, though I've never seen it before."

"Great!" I laugh. "And we have a cracked windowpane."

Darkness falls and distant Grangeville disappears. Zigzags of searing light blind us. The storm continues steadily toward us, throwing out one jagged bolt after another. I clutch the log to my chest. I feel Jack's fingers moving next to my leg, prodding the mattress. "What's wrong?" I say.

"Shit! There're fucking metal springs in our mattress." He rips the twin mattress out from beneath us, bedding and all, and tosses it onto the floor.

"Great!" I'm nearly overcome with nausea. I sit cross-legged on the hard plywood box serving as a platform for the mattress and lean close to Jack for protection. I know this will be the most dangerous storm we've experienced so far.

In the darkness, each volley of lightning peppers the forest in a prairie-wide swatch, blinding us like car lights on a lonely road. The strikes burst just seconds apart—a stampede rushing the tower. At one point, treetops burst into flames. Between bolts, the orange glow blazes higher. The entire forest catches. I think of the jet engine roar that a firefighter told me about. My fingers grip Jack's so tightly that I realize I'm hurting him. "What will we do? We're going to be trapped."

"Grab the cat and head east," Jack says. "Camp out on Pilot Knob until they put out the fire. They may have to airlift us out. But it's rocky up higher. It'd be almost impossible for the fire to burn past the ridge."

"I'm scared." My heart races as I calculate how much time we'll need before we head down to the Scout. At the rate it's coming, I imagine we'll have to leave shortly.

"Jude," I call. She meows from beneath the bedcovers Jack threw on the floor. "Should I grab a few things? Toothbrushes, pillows, cat food? My camera."

A series of bolts tear the night open. We can see a patch of prairie in the distance. The booming thunder crashes, echoing off nearby ridges. I close my eyes, resting them from the lightning's brilliance, the shape of the last bolt remaining emblazoned on my retinas. Another volley of strikes and another swatch of trees flame up. We can easily see the orange blaze between strikes now.

"Grab the cat," Jack says. "Let's get out of here."

I am just moving off the bed's platform when the rain starts; huge pelting drops spattering the windows, whipping around the sides of the tower, shaking the shutters, drenching the forest.

As it comes down, we realize our fate might not be sealed. The blazing evergreens are no longer visible after a while. The lightning slows to a bolt here and another one there, with lots of space between. Rain continues to drench the forest. My legs feel weak, but eventually we pull the mattress back onto the wooden box. I collapse onto it, pulling the covers over me. The rain pours all through the night. By morning, there is no fire in sight.

We linger in bed this morning, as the storm wore us out. The day looks fresh and the sky is mostly blue. You'd never even know we had such a terrifying storm. As we spoon beneath the warm covers, the tower begins to shake. My heart jumps. What now, an earthquake?

"What the fuck?" Jack says, rolling onto his back. He groans as he stretches. The tower shakes again. He sits up.

I jump out of bed, scampering outside in my birthday suit. The catwalk is drippy wet. I hurry to the prairie side of the tower and look over the rail. Down below is a giant moose scratching itself against the support beams. It rubs its thick hide back and forth and back and forth along the timbers. The tower shudders. I turn and wave for Jack to come outside.

He's at my side in a flash and together we lean over the railing, watching the huge brute of an animal scratch its hairy haunch. The sun rises over Pilot Knob. Birds sing. Water droplets drip from the trees, sparkling like crystals. The moose continues to scratch his dusty side against the stinky creosote-soaked beams.

Back inside, we eat breakfast. The moose is a good story, but the storm is a better one. I decide to write an article for the *Grangeville Tribune*. I sit down in the green chair with my tablet and pen.

I feel the need to get the facts down on paper, although my thinking is a bit scattered this morning. Besides describing what happened, I'm also making a grocery list in my mind, imagining a hot shower, and filling three washers with dirty clothes at the laundromat. Plus, the roads could be goose grease from all the rain. I press the pen to paper again, frowning at the whiff of BO rising from my armpits. Even though I'm wearing my cleanest dirty clothes, I stink.

Jack has been off and on the radio since breakfast, assuring the district that we are fine. Arizona calls it a "Terrible Storm." We feel stunned still, both by the noise and lightning flashes, and the hard rain that fell afterward. What luck to have a torrential rain extinguish the treetop fires. The rain fell heavier than we've seen so far. We're lucky the downpour came when it did, either that or we'd be waking on Pilot Knob this morning.

Over the radio, I hear Arizona say, *Sorry about the mattress. We'll get you a new one, and we'll fix that cracked pane. Tell Nance to just walk on in the trailer and use the shower when she gets here. Over and out.*

I finish the article and head out. The drive down the mountain is uneventful. Following along Elk River Road, I slow at what appears to be a slick corner. The road is good, but my mind isn't. Besides going stir-crazy, the storm really did frighten me. I bump along, replaying last night's lightning and thunder as I try to avoid potholes. Ball lightning, trees flaming up, and torrential rain pouring down was a nightmare, really. A flutter of fear flits through my chest.

But soon I'm walking along Grangeville's Main Street, feeling carefree in the wide-open space. The sun is hell-hot, and my blue halter top, cutoffs, and Dr. Scholl's wooden sandals are keeping me as cool as can be expected. Cowboys smile and nod at me. Men like me. I'm not sure why, though Jack says it's because I'm sexy. I'm not actually an exhibitionist like Mother said I was. I mean, yes, I'd been sunbathing in my bikini in the backyard when Jack drove up on his motorcycle when we were first dating. Yes, I kissed him in public. What was I supposed to do?

Shrugging away the memory, I turn into the newspaper building ready to deliver my story about the "Terrible Storm" with the ball lightning hovering above the prairie. Jack insisted that ball was just another transformer blowing. I said, "Transformers don't hover like that. Transformers blow like M-80s, accompanied by a huge flash of light." This ball of light appeared large even twenty-five miles away. In the pitch blackness, it raised off the ground and hovered there for a few moments, reminding me of Mother's story about ball lightning back home in Virginia.

When she was a girl, a ball of lightning rolled in the front door and out the back door. Lightning can do all sorts of strange things, even roll down the aisle of an airplane. They say there's a 1 in 3,000 chance of getting hit.

I feel cocky standing at the newspaper counter—we survived one of the worst storms Grangeville, Idaho, has seen in who knows when.

Dames with Comics
by Al Clover

I wish I could say it ended in a hail of gunfire, but I can't because it didn't.

The wet streets and cloudy skies make The Avenue a dangerous place. But I walk these streets anyways. Around each
building corner lurks—I'm sure—evil.... It rained overnight,
and the Ave is coming alive as the early morning bursts from
behind the cloudy skies. Heads down, the city's denizens
avoid puddles that dot the sidewalks as they scurry to their
destinations, determined to arrive without mishaps. The Ave,
as it's known by the locals, is in the heart of the U-District. It
is an eight-block-long melting pot of restaurants, bookstores,
coffee shops, and a tattoo parlor or two. My office—some call
it a shop—fits right in with the quirky nature of the area, offering a respite from the perilous Seattle streets.

As I round the corner, I smell the aroma of fried rice and
wonton soup. I pass Wong's Chinese Food Emporium.
Wong's has the best Chinese food in the city. Unfortunately,
it's also my kryptonite.

Wong stands in front of his restaurant's open door, enjoying a morning cigarette. "Good morning, Alex."

"Hey Wong, how's it going?"

"It's good, Alex. Wonton and fried rice for lunch today?"

"We'll see. Got a lot on my plate today. So many clients, so little time."

"Alright, well you know where I am if you need lunch."

Nodding in agreement and moving toward the door of my office, I see a Post-it note stuck to glass.

I look around—you can never be too watchful. I pull the note and read, "Come next door, I've got something for you."

Normally I'd hope this was an invitation to some fun…nudge-nudge, wink-wink…but being familiar with the handwriting and this particular perfume fragrance, I know it's business. The Ave's motor traffic plays a symphony in the background as I walk past my doorway and up to Inks Enough Tattoo Parlor just past my office. I'm curious as to what surprise awaits me.

Pushing the door open and removing my fedora (I'm a gentleman after all), I step into the parlor. I feel a palpable change in the air. Is this the beginning of another case?

Sheela Rocher, or "Rocker" as she prefers, is the proprietress. She is lovely, sporting full-sleeve tattoos and a back piece, which she only shows off in the summertime.

She's dressed in her usual leather miniskirt and black blouse with puffy sleeves. She stands in front of the counter opposite our connecting wall. Her hair is shaved three quarters on the left side and the rest sweeps over to reach just below her jaw line on the right. She looks very punk, but classy punk. With the tattoos, the punk hair, the leather, and a few piercings in each ear, I sometimes think of her as a pirate. A classy punk pirate. My eye is drawn to her chair-like apparatus in the middle of the room, which reminds me of the barbershop chair or maybe that of a dentist. You know, the kind that can be moved to an upright or reclined position depending on where the client needs the ink. I often hear cries of pain from Rocker's clients when I'm in the shop. I mean...the office. In the past Rocker has told me, with a devious smile on her face, the chair is where the magic happens. I believe her.

Her first customer is standing beside the chair, taking his shirt off. I ignore him as he settles in and reclines.

"Hey Rocker, what's up?" I always begin with a question. It helps get people talking.

"It's all good, Alex," she says, looking up and smiling in greeting. She points to the package sitting on the counter.

"Here, this was dropped off a little bit ago. The UPS guy was cute, so thank you for not being available to accept the delivery."

"And who was this again?" Can't be too careful. Rocker looks at me with a slight shake of her head, the same look clients give me sometimes when they're not sure what I'm asking. "Alex, you're weird."

"Hmm, how was it delivered?" I clarify. "Regular courier service? Was he wearing a uniform?"

"The usual way," she says, still shaking her head. "It's comic books, for your store. Like every delivery." She gestures toward the package.

"Okay, it's probably safe then."

"Uh-huh, okay. Alrighty then." Rocker isn't quite sure how to respond to my paranoia. "So...anyway, I signed for it, so it's all yours."

"Thanx. I'd better get to the office in case a client needs me."

Rocker waves good-bye as I step back onto The Ave with my package and I hear her say to her client, "Owns the store next door. Thinks he's a superhero private eye, though."

The package is heavy and well-wrapped, and when I shake it there is no movement nor sound from the contents. Returning to my office door, I insert the key and, as usual, it sticks. I twist and turn the key in the lock, trying to convince it to co-operate. Success! I push the door open and step across the threshold. The space is dim, but the light switch is next to the door and, with my free hand, I turn on the lights. Placing the package on the desk, I cross to the window and pull up the shades. It's raining again. I turn and look in the direction of the front door. I know that when a client enters in the morning hours and looks at me sitting at my desk, they just see my silhouette, the sun—when there is some—gives me a shining aura. Makes it hard to look directly at me. To my benefit, a streetlight was put in outside my window, strategically giving the same effect to evening clients.

On my desk, close at hand in a prominent position, stands a half-full bottle of Old Grand Dad bourbon and an empty glass. They tempt me, as if waiting for my hand to grasp the bottle and pour out a shot to get the day started. *Nah, too early.* Around the bottle and glass, files are left scattered all over my desk. Some part of me knows these are just invoices I need to pay, but I imagine they are my current cases. In the mornings, before anyone walks in the door, I can be whoever I want to be, right?

Opposite the bottle is a three-tier stacking tray which the files should be occupying, but my filing system balked with disgust at my arrogance. The files proudly ignore that stacking tray. Directly in front of me is a chair for my clients. It's old,

wooden, and uncomfortable by design. My clients can sometimes ramble, the chair helps them focus and get on with
telling me their problems. From where they sit, they can see,
hanging to the right of my desk, a picture of a man dressed in
a pin-striped suit looking wistful. Don't know who the man is,
but I liked the wooden frame and the picture is just a place-
holder for my own photo choice. As the gentleman featured is
older, everyone assumes he was my partner, who was, perhaps, killed investigating a case. I don't dissuade them of the
notion. "I avenged his death," I tell any client who inquires. I
tell you, it impresses every time.

The wall on the left behind me is dominated by a black
four-drawer file cabinet that holds all my case files and a pot-
ted cactus. The plant looks to be almost dead but don't let that
fool you—it'll bite you if you get near it. The prickly bastard
was given to me by a former client. She gave it to me after I
solved her rather complicated case, said it matched my prickly
attitude. In her honor, I named the cactus Pocky. Leaning
against this plant is my Nick Fury action figure. Just to be
clear, it's an action figure not a toy.

Nick Fury is my mentor. He taught me everything I know.
Not that Nick Fury is a private eye—or a comic bookstore
owner—but his valor and his determination speak to me. He's
also really a cool cat. I guess I could replace the anonymous
photo of the guy in pinstripes with a graphic of Fury; I'll have
to think on that.

As I sit at my desk, the sun warming my back, I go over a
"case file" I randomly select. Then I hear the door open,
bringing with it the sounds of The Ave traffic speeding toward
mid-morning. I look up. A client.

He's young, probably in his early twenties. With a wrinkled brow, he hesitates, then steps all the way in. His light blue windbreaker is wet and reflects the light. As he removes his baseball cap, I see brown hair, damp from the recent rain. His tan is obviously from another location on the globe. Seattle has been sunless for a couple of weeks. His uncertain movements show he's questioning his decision to hire a private detective. Standing where he is just inside the door, he peers into each corner of the room—searching for what, I don't know. As the office is brightly lit, any hidden adversaries would be visible. And then he jumps at the squeak of his own tennis shoes—he must be in trouble. I'm sure of it.

"How can I help you?" Always start with a question, remember?

I see him glance at the Old Grand Dad. I'd offer him a shot, it looks like he could use it, but it's nine o'clock in the morning. Even for me that's too early for Grand Dad. Then again, somewhere in the world it's five o'clock and if he asks for a drink, I won't judge. I've had days like that.

I can tell this guy needs to talk. He's sweating. I can see drips of sweat collecting on his nose—that can't be from the rain. Obviously, he's nervous. Most of my clients don't sweat, but the ones that do...whew!

"Umm, ah," he stutters and then starts over. "Okay, I've never done this before. I'll just jump right in. I'd like you to find a comic for me." He looks everywhere except at me, rubbing the back of his neck.

Looks like it's time for me to put on my metaphorical fedora. "So, what'd this comic do to you? Tell a bad joke?"

If I had a clock in the office, you'd hear the seconds ticking away in the silence. He looks at me just like Rocker did twenty minutes ago.

"What?"

If this were a movie, the screen would do that thing where it shimmers as I stand there in my comic book store with the counter covered in comics. I come back to reality every morning with my first customer. The box I retrieved from Rocker is still sitting on my desk unopened, most likely the back issues I ordered from another comic store. I move the package down behind the counter. I give the guy a friendly smile.

"Sorry, how can I help you?"

"As I said…I'm looking for a comic."

"Well you chose wisely. The Comics Clubhouse at your service. Whatcha looking for?"

"Umm, Batman comics?"

"Which one?"

"I need the one where Alfred dresses up like Batman, so Bruce Wayne can fool the Joker."

I know exactly what he's talking about. But first I grab a stack of single-fold paper towels from behind the counter. "Let's dry those wet hands first, before you touch anything.…"

"Sorry," he says, drying his hands. He hesitates for a moment, not knowing what to do with the paper towel. Taking it from him, I stuff it in my back pocket. You never know when you might need a DNA sample. Just sayin'.

I lead him over to the floor bins containing all of the Batman back issues and, before he can drag his wet sleeve across the comics, I pull one out to show him.

"Is this the one you're looking for?"

He gingerly picks it up and admires the cover which depicts Batman swinging across the Gotham rooftops, the Joker shaking his fist at the Bat.

"This is the one!" With that he goes from the downtrodden, drowned rat façade to the gleeful look of a kid who just found his missing puppy. "I knew the Comics Clubhouse was my best shot!"

"Well thanx, that's a nice compliment." As I say that, I notice what looks to be a Green Lantern T-shirt peeking from under his jacket, a rounded white shape against a Kelly green fabric.

"Hey, cool T-shirt." I'm seeing another money-making possibility. "Which Green Lantern do you like? Hal Jordan? Or are you old-school and like Alan Scott?" He's now got a surprised look on his face replacing his confusion from earlier. "Of course, Guy Gardner is my fave, especially during the '90s when he was seriously funny. Keith Giffen and JM DeMatteis were quite the comedic duo."

"Hey, good guess," he says running his finger under the collar of his jacket further exposing the T-shirt. Looking down he grins, "Yeah, I'm a big fan of Alan Scott. The idea of his power being susceptible to wood as opposed to Hal Jordan's inability to affect anything that was the color yellow just makes more sense to me. Also, I like that his ring is powered by magic, not some giant space battery."

"Hey, so I just happened to get some older Green Lantern comics in and, if I remember, there are some Alan Scott issues. Wanna take a look?"

"Oh man, that's great! I've been looking for some issues to complete my collection."

I lead him back to the front of the store. Slipping behind the counter I grab the package and rip it open, pulling out the older Green Lantern issues.

"Oh yeah, I was right. All from the 1940s. They're not mint but still in mid-grade for condition."

Forgetting to be not-a-nerd, he hops from one foot to the other as I lay them out. "This is great," he gushes, picking up one of the issues and, with a fist pump, he looks at me with a huge grin. "I've been looking for this issue for so long. I thought I'd never complete my collection! Dude, this gives me a solid run from beginning to end! Wow, this is so cool."

"Excellent, I'm glad to help you finish a run. You need any other issues?" My salesman's hat has replaced my fedora and is firmly planted on my head.

"Yes, but I need to check my list. Since I wasn't thinking about Green Lantern issues, I left it at home. I'll just go home and grab it." Gotta love his enthusiasm. "I'll be back in, like, twenty minutes."

"No worries. You don't have to come right back. Check your list at home and then just call me. If I have the issues, I'll hold them for you. And if I don't have them in stock, I can use my online database to do some detective work. I can probably find some of the issues by next week, but it may take longer." I grab a business card from the metal mesh cardholder on the counter. "Here's my card. Just give me a call. Let's finish your Green Lantern run."

"This is awesome." He pulls out his wallet and hands me his credit card to pay for his Batman and Green Lantern comics.

I keep the salesman hat on as I run his card for the purchase. "Just remember The Comics Clubhouse next time you're looking to complete a run. If I don't have it, I will find it, guaranteed."

My cash register is happy, I'm happy, and my customer is happy.

"Thanks again!" he calls, as he braves the rain with his comics safely stored in a plastic bag under his arm.

When I'm alone in the store again, I find my way back behind my desk. The thrill of a sale stays with me for a while, and then my mind drifts to a case I'd like to solve. The case of a beautiful woman with no-good husband. Maybe she would need someone with wit and wisdom to find out he's swindled her family out of a fortune. Maybe I'm the P.I. for the job. As I drift into the noir fantasy the weather cooperates as the skies open up and begin to dump the proverbial Washingtonian liquid sunshine we're so well known for.

After a lunch of Wonton soup and fried rice, I go about my usual routine, helping one customer find that elusive back issue, debating with another about who is stronger—Superman or the Hulk—and ringing up sales. As my thirty-third customer leaves, something catches my eye. Or should I say, *someone*.

I notice her because she walks by slowly, peering in the windows. She hesitates at one end of the storefront and then circles back to the door. Any ordinary Seattleite jets inside to escape the rain. But not her. She's cautious. Good for her.

As she enters, she swipes her blonde locks out of her eyes. I've never seen her before. I'm not one of those guys who wolf-whistles at a pretty woman, but I'm also not one who doesn't notice a good-looking dame.

"Hi," I say, "Welcome to The Comics Clubhouse."

"I—" Her voice is quiet, "I'm looking for the owner," she says, looking around.

"Cool. That would be me." I admit, my pulse quickens.

"Oh, good." Her voice grows louder. "I have some comics and I was hoping to have someone look at them."

"I'd be happy to, why don't you bring them in tomorrow?"

"Oh, well…," she pauses, "There are quite a few boxes in the Comics Library. Actually, too many to bring in."

The Comics Library? It's capitalized in my head. Fedora-hat time. I look at her more closely. I normally wouldn't have expected to see her in the store, she's not wearing a cartoon T-shirt and she certainly *has* taken a shower in the last twenty-four hours. Why then would *she* have so many comics? First up, she's dressed in a nice blue coat and I can see her skirt is a similar blue and it's just above the knee. Business profession-al? Her blonde hair is mid-length and looks well cared for. Earrings and a diamond ring, along with the hair, make me think money, but she doesn't flaunt it. Rather understated. "Alright. Can you tell me more about this Comics Library, if you don't mind?"

"Well, it was my uncle's. He was big collector of comics, and he passed away last year."

"Oh, I'm sorry." Uncle? Large batch of comics? Who was this guy? "So, you're talking maybe twenty or thirty boxes?"

"No. It's, well…it's more like he took all of the walls out of the second floor of our house and he stored them there."

I hope my mouth doesn't drop too far. "Oh. Well then, okay. Yes, I guess I could come and take a look."

"My husband isn't keen on the whole situation," she says. "I'd like you to come when he's not home."

I nod and stick out my hand to shake hers. "My name is Alex Carter. I'm the owner here at The Comics Clubhouse."

Losing Control
by Lisa Dailey

I remember reading that the difference between fear and excitement was about two inches—the physical distance between the place where fear tends to tie your stomach in knots and the place where butterflies flitter about in excitement. Though both emotions have the same physiological effect on the body.

During the six-hour bus ride from Vietnam to Cambodia my fear held the butterflies struggling to take flight captive. Even after three months of international travel, entering a new country continued to produce anxiety. I closed my eyes and focused on relaxing, hoping that by calming my body, my mind would follow. My fear was a biological response to help me deal with the unknown and the irrational terrors that continued to circulate in my mind. But what danger was I facing?

Three months earlier, I sat with my husband, Ray, and our two teenage boys, RJ and Tyler, in a California airport and decided to face my fears and embark on this journey because returning to a life filled with grief and self-doubt where I was struggling to function was far more terrifying. But I still hadn't been able to fully release fear's grip. Losing seven family members in five years, including my mom, dad, and twenty-five-year-old brother, had instilled a belief that everyone close to me was being systematically taken away. And my relationship with my mother had been complicated. Her passing in particular left me reverberating with her criticism, which weighed heavily on me still.

Now, reclined in the plush seat of the tour bus, I tried to convince myself to act out of a place of excitement rather than fear. In Cambodia, I would look at my life and be excited by the possibilities, act with determination, and feel confident I was making informed choices. It was time to reclaim my confidence, return to my sense of self.

We arrived in Phnom Penh, the capital of Cambodia, and found a tuk-tuk to take us to our hotel. The boys were excited to ride in the three-wheeled motorized vehicle with a motorcycle in the front and a covered carriage for passengers in the back. Nothing went wrong—our luggage was not lost, we were safe and made it to the hotel without issue. I still felt out of place, but rather than letting dread rule the day, I embraced my unease and paid more attention to my surroundings.

Compared to cities in Vietnam, Phnom Penh was less developed—the streets worn down and strewn with garbage. Many roads were dirt and even in this capital city the buildings were old and dilapidated. Perhaps after almost two months, I'd adapted to the pace and rhythm of my surroundings in Vietnam only to jump into a new adventure, and I missed the familiarity I'd left behind.

We settled into our hotel and Ray and I began the now familiar process of researching what kinds of adventures we could have.

"How long do you want to stay in Phnom Penh?" I asked Ray as we searched the Internet.

"I don't know. Why?"

"I'm just trying to look forward to the adventures rather than letting the new country jitters take over," I said. "Having a bit of a plan helps."

"You'll be fine." Ray flashed a cursory smirk and went right back to his research. "Look at this," he said, turning his laptop toward me. I looked at the website he'd found then we exchanged a knowing glance. Ray had just found an experience not to be missed by two teenage boys.

"Oh, we have to go there."

Without telling the kids too much, Ray and I took the boys to lunch at a place specializing in rural Cambodian cuisine. The restaurant served as a training ground for former street youth and other marginalized and at-risk groups. The goal for student staff was to learn new skills that would allow them to get into the workforce and improve their lives.

As soon as we were seated, I made sure RJ and Tyler both saw tarantula on the menu. After an initial shock, the boys were game to try the deep-fried spider appetizer.

"What do they taste like?" RJ asked the waitress as we placed our order.

"Chicken," the waitress said without missing a beat.

None of us expected her next question, "Do you want to see the live tarantulas?"

"Like, before they're cooked?" Ray asked.

"Yes. We have some you can hold," she replied.

"Um. Okay," Ray answered with mixed anticipation and hesitation before I could even wrap my mind around being at the same table with live tarantulas. Deep fried tarantulas were one thing. Live, gigantic, furry spiders mere inches from my person were another.

The waitress returned to our table a few minutes later with a small white saucer and upside-down cup in hand. She set the plate on the table and then lifted the cup to reveal two tarantulas the size of eggs cuddled together with their spindly, black legs intertwined. The spiders were completely still on the saucer and we couldn't tell if they were alive or dead. Perhaps they were in shock from seeing their cousins dropped into pools of bubbling oil.

"Are they alive?" I asked, wondering aloud what we all feared.

"Yes." She picked one up and held it out for us to take.

My adrenaline spiked as Ray tentatively extended his hand, while asking, "Is it safe? Do they bite?"

"Only if threatened. But their venom is weak." She placed one spider and then the second in Ray's open hands, none of us questioning her definition of "weak."

I've never been particularly fond of spiders. The spiders I'm used to, however, are smaller than a dime and don't have fangs, at least not that I could see without a microscope. These tarantulas were far too close for my comfort. With an urge to scream, I backed my chair away from the table with a jerk. I hurried to the other side to put some extra distance between me and the hairy beasts. Now far enough away from the small monsters, I pulled out my camera to document the dread creeping over Ray's face as one spider crawled up his arm, headed right for the gap between his sleeve and flesh, perhaps to nestle in the warmth of his armpit.

"Okay, you can take them back," Ray said, his eyes imploring the waitress to remove the spiders. She gently lifted the spiders from his arms and cradled them in her hands.

"Does anyone else want to hold them?" She showed no discomfort whatsoever as she offered the spiders to each of us in turn. I guessed she had faced far scarier things in her life than a spider crawling up her arm.

Our heads all shook in unison. There was no way the rest of us would touch those spiders.

"Where do you get them?" Ray asked.

"Suppliers capture the tarantulas in the jungle," she replied. "People in the jungle eat them all the time."

A few minutes later, the waitress returned with a plate of three deep-fried tarantulas and a side of black pepper lime sauce. I couldn't help but wonder who determined that black pepper and lime were the perfect accompaniment to tarantula.

We each broke off a deep brown leg, dipped it in the sweet, tangy sauce and tentatively bit into the appendage. They had the crunch and taste of overcooked French fries. Then we turned to the spider's abdomen.

When cutting the rubbery body part proved futile, Ray and Ty each took hold of a spider belly and popped the whole thing into their mouths in one go. They chewed and chewed and finally grabbed their drinks and washed down the masticated bodies.

"Well?" I asked.

"Definitely didn't taste like chicken," Ray said with flecks of the black body and hair lodged between his teeth.

"More like digested insects," Tyler added.

"Not super enjoyable, but not altogether disgusting either," Ray said.

I couldn't help but notice how we were all growing on this adventure. Not even a month before, Tyler was hesitant to sit among the crowds in Hanoi to eat. Now he was eating deep-fried tarantula. Even RJ, although equally hesitant to hold a tarantula as he had been to hold a scorpion back in Malaysia, wasted no time in breaking off a leg and giving it a taste test.

When the rest of our meal arrived, we all took turns trying the red tree ant soup. Compared to the earthy, bug-infested, grittiness of the tarantula, the soup was a delightful combination of cucumber and lemon flavors. The ants didn't have much taste, but they added a pleasant, rice-like texture to the soup.

Returning to the hotel, we chalked the day up as a success and planned the next legs of our journey.

Breaking up the ten-hour bus ride from Phnom Penh to Siem Reap the next day, we stopped in a small, out-of-the-way, French colonial town called Battambang. Based on our limited Internet-knowledge, we expected to be met by a pack of kids looking to pick our pockets when we got off the bus. What we were not warned about were the blaring music videos sung by Cambodia's version of John Denver playing at max volume for the entire five-hour bus ride. By the time we hit Battambang, we didn't care what was left in our pockets to pilfer through, we just wanted off the bus.

When the bus pulled up to the drop-off point, there were no kids in sight, only a group of tuk-tuk drivers ready to deliver passengers to their chosen hotels. Drivers had their rates posted on their vehicles. From my window seat, I made eye contact with a driver and waved him over.

Stepping off the bus, I handed my backpack to the driver as Ray looked on.

"No, wait." Ray shook his head and put up a hand to stop me. "Lisa, what are you doing?"

"It's okay." I took Ray's hand. "He'll take us to our hotel."

"But we haven't negotiated the price. The website I looked at said they could charge us way too much," Ray protested.

"It's okay," I repeated. "His rate was posted on his tuk-tuk. It's two dollars. We're all good."

Ray had failed to notice the drivers, their posted rates, and my silent conversation of eye contact and nods with the driver as we arrived. I smiled, congratulating myself on my calm and collected demeanor. How was I the centered one for once?

Once at our hotel, we unloaded our backpacks. Yaya, the tuk-tuk driver and Battambang tour guide, showed us a brochure with local activities and we arranged for a pick up later that afternoon.

As the sun started its descent, Yaya returned to gather us for an evening tour of the killing caves. As the tuk-tuk chugged along the flat expanse of the Cambodian rice fields, larger vehicles flashing past us, Yaya explained he used to be a guide at the killing caves, and he was learning more about the history of Cambodia in his college classes. A lone limestone mountain, seemingly out of place in the otherwise flat landscape, edged ever closer as we spoke. Since dusk was not far off, we opted to drive to the top of the mountain rather than take the thirteen hundred steps. After passing people drenched in sweat on the way up, I was confident we'd made the right choice. Three spires of a Buddhist temple topped the peak. A row of golden Buddha statues draped in saffron robes perched on a stone wall looking out over the flat rice fields far below.

We walked through the trees to the top of the caves, startled on occasion by macaque monkeys jumping from tree to tree overhead, on the lookout for any food or shiny objects they could snag from unsuspecting tourists. Standing near three gaping holes in the mountain, Yaya explained, "The Khmer Rouge would take people to these caves and throw them in. Sometimes they would cut off their heads or stab the people before pushing them over the edge. One cave was for women, one for men, and the third for children. Some people survived the sixty-foot fall but died later from injuries or from having no food and water." Yaya paused before continuing, his features tightening. "The Khmer Rouge were most cruel to babies. They would smash the babies' heads against this large rock and then toss them down into the childrens' cave." A shiver ran through my body as I looked at the boulder, the middle stained dark with what I imagined had to be blood.

I glanced at RJ and Tyler to gauge how they were handling this information and saw they both looked shocked to hear about the brutality that occurred here. When Ray and I decided on a tour of the killing caves, I had hoped for a history lesson. I wanted the boys to know about the Cambodian genocide, to feel and understand the suffering that took place here. And although reading about the Cambodian genocide in a world history class would have nowhere near the impact as standing in the very place the atrocity occurred, I now considered that this might be too much for them. Even though I had learned about the Khmer Rouge in school, I had never imagined anything this brutal. Still, I was committed to stretching us all into a deeper understanding of world history, and I tried not to be too hard on myself over the choice to explore this area.

After a moment of silence, Yaya led us to the base of the killing caves. We followed several other groups down a long limestone stairway carved into the hill. Everyone was silent as we all held our collective breath out of respect for those who had been killed here and the brutality they suffered. Green vegetation and low-hanging vines covered the rock walls, adding to the closed-in stillness all around us. A huge golden Buddha reclined on his side in the center of the large cave interior. A smaller room opened to the side where a glass enclosure, the size of a large elevator, was filled with human skulls. Looking up, we could see the hole in the cave's ceiling where we had just stood and traced the victims' paths as they took their last breaths before hitting the stone floor, right where we were standing now. The atrocities that had taken place in this beautiful spot suddenly became all too real and emotionally overwhelming. RJ and Tyler, each caught up in the heaviness of the moment, moved closer on either side of me and I took hold of their hands and squeezed, reassuring them I was present. Learning to be present with loss was, after all, what had inspired me to embark on this journey with my family.

Yaya directed us out of the cave and led us to a rocky outcrop to watch the sun set and let the crisp greens and browns of the landscape and the brilliant oranges, pinks, and purples of the sunset calm our hearts and minds. We spread out on the rocks, each of us giving one another some space to digest the experience in our own way. I thought of the deaths in my own life and let my grief in for a few deep breaths. I looked at Yaya in silhouette on a rock with praying hands in front of his chest, his head bowed. I wondered how difficult it was for him to repeat this story day after day. Perhaps this prayer after the tour was his way of flushing the bad memories and returning to strength. In his own way, Yaya was giving me a new appreciation for not only the struggle of the Cambodian people, but the way in which they now made their way through the world—connecting to and understanding the atrocities of the past, but not letting the actions of the Khmer Rouge continue to instill fear.

As the sun's last rays disappeared, Yaya drove us to the base of the mountain and parked the tuk-tuk along the road where another immense cave, its entrance a hundred-foot fissure in the limestone mountain, swarmed with millions of winged creatures very much alive.

This single mountain in an otherwise flat landscape was home to extraordinary death and miraculous life. Cambodia continued to strike me as a place of duality—life and death, war and peace, chaos and harmony.

As the sky darkened, we sat on a rock wall and waited with a group of a hundred other tourists for the bats to head out on their nightly foray. Each time the boys spied a bat leaving the cave, they pointed it out, excited this might be the start of the exodus.

"Just wait," Yaya said, "you'll know when it really starts."

And sure enough, we watched a single bat be joined by two more and then twenty and then two hundred, ten thousand. The bats were departing the cool of their cave en masse. We stared at the sky in awe as millions of bats poured out of the rugged mouth in a twisting and churning column, seemingly apart but always together, setting off in a line across the sky to eat their fill of insects.

The bats have no control over their environment; they exist and hunt according to the setting of the sun, their own internal instinct. They rely on themselves and one another, each creature playing a part in the strength of the colony, helping to keep it functioning.

"Keep your mouths closed unless you want to sample the bat nectar," Yaya said, reminding us that the droplets falling from the sky were not sprinkles of rain dotting our faces.

Riding back to our hotel, we looked out over the land and could see the line of bats stretching for miles, as far as we could see, in the fading light. They flew on, not turning back until they'd had their fill or until the dawn came again, not dwelling on the past or fearing the future, but living only in the moment.

In contrast to Battambang where there were few tourists, we discovered the next day that Siem Reap was a tourist mecca. People from around the world flocked to see the Angkor Archaeological Park, just four miles north of the city on a site measuring over four hundred acres. I was ecstatic to be visiting Siem Reap, a place I had dreamed of visiting for as long as I could remember.

I had read about the Angkor temples when I was young, pouring over each page of a *National Geographic* magazine, studying each curve in the carved sandstone buildings, tracing each tree root growing on top of and through the walls, imagining myself standing in awe of the architecture and the gigantic trees towering above me in the jungle. I read the accompanying descriptions over and over, memorizing as many details as I could about this mysterious place.

The Angkor site was spread out over such a large area, it would have been impossible to see everything in a single day, so we purchased a three-day pass. Our tuk-tuk driver would often drop us off at a temple and indicate where he would pick us up, typically on the opposite side, allowing us to walk through the buildings at our leisure, climb to the top of some and look out at the surrounding jungle. The architecture was like nothing I'd ever seen. Nearly every surface was ornately decorated with a bas-relief frieze: carvings of *apsaras* (female spirits of the clouds and waters in Hindu and Buddhist culture) and *devatas* (stone carvings of males and females representing forest spirits, village gods, keepers of river crossings, caves, and mountains). Large holes dotted the walls where rubies, emeralds, and sapphires once glimmered in candle-lit passageways.

I had a hard time trying to wrap my mind around the fact that these structures were almost a thousand years old, constructed some eight hundred years before Lewis and Clark set out on their two-year trek from St. Louis to the West Coast of North America. The buildings were more than six hundred years older than my entire country.

Angkor Wat, the central temple in the complex and only one of hundreds in the area, was built in the early twelfth century and was still a significant religious center and a symbol of Cambodia, even appearing on its currency and national flag. The temple was surrounded by a moat, a consistent thirty-nine-foot wide ditch representing the oceans surrounding the world. Moving inward from the moat, a fifteen-foot high stone wall surrounded the temple. Three rectangular galleries, one built on top of the next, were designed as a pyramid representing the structure of the universe. The highest level represented Mount Meru, the home of the Hindu gods. At the center of the galleries stood five towers, representing the five peaks of the mountain, the center tower reaching nearly seventy feet into the air. In 1586, Antonio da Madalena, a Portuguese friar said, "[Angkor Wat] is of such extraordinary construction that it is not possible to describe it with a pen, particularly since it is like no other building in the world. It has towers and decoration and all the refinements which the human genius can conceive of."

Of the many temples we visited in the Angkor complex, my favorite by far was Bayon. The most distinctive features of this temple were the two hundred sixteen serene stone faces jutting out from the otherwise flat towers, smiling down upon me. While there is debate whether the faces represent Buddha or King Jayavarman VII, all the faces have the same calming effect on the onlookers. I felt a new sense of peacefulness as I wandered through the temple.

Feeling negative or unworthy in this tranquil environment was impossible. The faces served as an incredibly powerful reminder that I was worthy, I could hear my inner voice telling me I would be okay, and that I was enough.

As I looked up at the faces—weathered grey stone against a blue sky—I knew I had to let go of my fears. I had to stop beating myself up for not being what someone else thought I should be or for what my late mother had told me I wasn't. Now that both of my parents were gone, the only way left to experience this connection between parent and child would be with my own children. To look upon them lovingly and unconditionally with no expectation or need to control them. To give them the voice of reassurance that could echo in their minds. To be present.

I gazed into the stone carving and relaxed my stomach, letting the butterflies free to flitter about, releasing fear and embracing excitement. I would no longer repeat the story of not being good enough, not doing things right. I was ready for a new story. I was meant to be here. Now. Standing among the faces of Bayon Temple and letting the power of the two hundred sixteen faces smiling down upon me sink into every pore.

Unbearably Beautiful
by Seán Dwyer

Bloomington

Rita worried that this trip might become unbearably beautiful. The trees lining the two-lane highway still sported small, spring-green leaves. The young man chauffeuring her in her Honda Accord kept the speedometer needle at a steady fifty-eight. There was no hurry. The engine, used to city streets, hummed with joy at its liberation. New tires sang as they embraced the asphalt in the smooth curves buried among the hills of south-central Indiana.

In a crate in the backseat, the driver's rat terrier pup, Madra, was sniffing the breeze blowing through Rita's open window. Gas mileage be darned; Madra deserved all the smells he could gather. His mouth hung open, his tongue flicking the odors, his eyes closed against the sun. He made small peeps of joy.

In the driver's seat, Kyle R. Lane—the best painter Rita knew—mirrored Madra's smile, as well as her own. Swirling air caught his long, black curls and wrapped his hair around his face. She couldn't see his blue eyes behind his dark glasses, but she imagined them open wide with the wonder of getting away from Bloomington's college-town vibe to spend the summer painting in the Southwest. The plan was to drop her off at the hospice her friend Cynthia owned and operated in Cardiff-by-the-Sea in California and then for him to backtrack to New Mexico, where he would paint for a month. He was to return to retrieve her to take her back to Bloomington for the academic year.

Yes, this experience would be unbearably beautiful. A blend of the joy of a road trip and the pain of leaving Bloomington behind forever. Kyle, her favorite customer in her art-supply store, had no idea she was going to stay in California when they finally reached the coast. Today was not the day to tell him she was not just visiting Cynthia at the hospice but was going to work there until ovarian cancer, at bay but lurking in Rita's belly, killed her. *Unbearably beautiful.*

Driving through Ellettsville and Spencer slowed their pace, but the towns also marked distance between Rita and her oncologist, as well as the friends who had urged her to keep fighting her disease. Distance brought her a peace that would surely grow the farther west they drove.

At a traffic light in Spencer, Madra sniffed and started to whine. He stood on his hind legs, nose pressed against the wire wall of his crate. Rita looked around but saw no other dogs in the street outside the car.

"You see the Golden Arches, boy?" Kyle said. Madra yipped. "I'm sorry, sweetie. No McDonald's today."

Rita raised her eyebrows. "You eat there? You feed Madra there?"

"Sometimes, when I have paint on my hands and don't want to mess with turpentine, I take Madra there instead of cooking. He gets one bite of a cheeseburger and a French fry." The light changed, and he drove past the McDonald's on the corner.

"He recognizes the building?"

"He's a smart boy, my Madra."

She knew how bright he was. Kyle had started bringing Madra to Moody Blue Art Supply when he was two months old and only mostly potty trained. Rita and her business partner, Kathy, had fallen in love with the little white-and-black speck of energy. As he grew, he showed off tricks Kyle had taught him, from sitting to playing dead when Kyle pointed a paintbrush at him.

Madra tracked the restaurant as it receded from view. When he lost sight of it, he lay down, his chin on his paws, and sighed.

"You just had breakfast, you greedy goofball," Kyle said. He turned to Rita. "Don't be like me and spoil him. He'll ride you without mercy."

"I'm still processing your McDonald's habit. I usually see you buying hippie food at the Co-op."

"Sure, but I'm twenty-eight. I still feel invulnerable to danger." He turned his face toward her, eyes still on the road, then glanced at her and smiled, a dimple emerging on his cheek. Rita and Kathy sometimes commented on that dimple after Kyle left their store.

"Well, I'm forty-five, and I know that stuff will kill you slowly."

"You must not eat there, because I wouldn't have guessed you were even forty."

"You're so gallant."

Kyle merged onto I-70 just east of Terre Haute, joining the disjointed convoy of semis headed toward Illinois. Rita hated the boxed-in sensation of driving in the slow lane between two semis, with another crawling past her on the left. With Kyle at the wheel, she could relax enough to compare this college town to the one where she lived. *Had lived*, she reminded herself. She wasn't even sure she would come back to sell her house—

"No!" Kyle's yell alerted her just before he punched the brakes, flinging her into the shoulder belt. A gold Lexus squeezed into their lane, unaware that its bumper wasn't going to clear theirs. Kyle managed to give it an inch of passing room, risking at the same time contact with the semi on their tail.

At the same moment, Rita heard a thump in the backseat, and Madra yelped, then began to howl. While Kyle steadied the car, she turned and knelt on the seat. Madra lay on his back, flailing to regain his footing. He caught her eye and gave her a piteous moan.

"Just a sec, sweetie," she told him. "Kyle, can you pull off at the next exit?"

"No problem." He turned onto US 41 and found a gas station. Rita hopped out of the car and opened the back door. The driver's door closed, and Kyle's steps crunched as he trotted around the car. She unhooked the door to the crate and helped Madra stand. He shook himself from head to tail and gave her a grateful lick on the mouth.

"Pfft, Madra, thank you, baby. Are you okay?"

Madra's yelps gave way to happy whimpers. Kyle leaned over her shoulder, brushing against her back. She shivered with a mix of delight and dread.

"I'm sorry, buddy," Kyle said, his voice cracking. He reached out, and Madra licked his hand. "Daddy didn't hook you up tight enough." He stood upright, as did Rita. "Still seven miles to go in Indiana, and I already hurt my dog. I really should have boarded him with my parents."

Rita patted him on the shoulder. "Hey, I was the one who said you should bring him along. If you couldn't leave him in his home, the best thing for him was to be with you."

"You were pretty relentless about my abandoning him."

"I have abandonment issues. Don't we all? I was projecting."

"And you were right, I'm sure."

"When I at least *think* I'm right, I'm tenacious." She leaned forward and found herself almost nose to nose with him. As they both paused to take a breath, his seriousness made her smile, then giggle. Kyle burst out laughing.

"You're always so gentle in your store. Are you going to boss me around the whole trip?"

She paused. "Some of the way, anyway. I figure you'll start pushing back at some point."

They turned to Madra. "I'll have to strap him in tighter," Kyle said.

Madra raised his eyebrows. Rita shook her head. "How about you let him sit with me? I can help steady him if you stop hard."

"They say dogs become projectiles in a car."

"I'll connect his harness to my shoulder belt."

Kyle pursed his lips and exhaled. "Final objection. He'll get heavy."

"Final reminder. I said to bring him instead of driving him to your parents' house. I have to live with my decisions. When is lunch?"

Kyle started. "Did you skip breakfast?"

"Nah. But Illinois is a wasteland. Just wondering if we have a plan."

"I always stop in Vandalia. Chuck Wagon Café. Have you been there?"

She shook her head. "I haven't been that far on I-70. Sounds adventurous. Let's do it." She scooped up Madra and plopped him on her lap in the front seat. Kyle closed the back door and circled back to the other side of the car. When Rita had Madra's harness entwined in her belt, Kyle took the ramp back onto I-70.

Madra stood on Rita's thighs, his tiny paws trembling when the car swayed, but he panted with excitement as they drove past the few trees on the prairie. Every couple of miles he turned to Rita and gave her a grateful slurp on the cheek. She would have to remember to wash her face, as well as her hands, when they reached Vandalia.

Just before the Effingham exit, Kyle asked, "Do you need to stop before Vandalia? It's another half-hour." Rita didn't answer, and he looked over at her. Her head lay against the door frame, and Madra had curled up and tucked his muzzle under her chin. If it were legal to pull out his phone, he would take a photo of them. It would be sweet enough to risk running off the road.

The pic would also help him with the portrait he was painting of Rita. It was a surprise for her, so he couldn't ask her to pose. He had spent much of the two weeks since they decided to travel together working on the screened-in back porch of his house, capturing her as he saw her at Moody Blue Art Supply: her honey eyes, her wry smile, her light-brown hair.

He enjoyed painting assignments for his MFA courses, but the work he did for love, like his Ireland landscapes and his series of Madra as he grew, transported his mind to a zone where nothing could distract it from the simple act of dipping a brush in a dab of paint. The carnal joy of feeling the brush rasp against the canvas often made him shiver. The broad background strokes in a light aqua to match the wall behind the sales counter at the store, the finer swoops to define Rita's jawline and her lips, the delicate tinting involved in capturing her eye color, the entire process served to remind him that he had been built to serve a purpose that brought more joy than utility to the world.

Rita was a painter herself, and Kyle could not understand how she had been able to set down her brush to become a conduit of support to other artists. She had admitted shyly that the one painting displayed in the store was her work. Rita had painted the portrait of her business partner, Kathy Lodge, when she was an undergrad at Indiana, before choosing an MBA over an MFA. A youthful Kathy surveyed the store, captured in time at her graduation with her own BFA. Kyle had asked Kathy why none of her own work hung at the store, and Kathy had replied that her rendering of Rita did her no justice. That was why *she* had chosen the MBA route.

Kyle turned on the stereo. He had brought along numerous USB drives with enormous playlists, and the current one held every Top 40 hit from the 1980s, the decade he assumed most resonated with Rita. He increased the volume slowly, and Rita finally stirred. Out of the corner of his eye, he saw her eyes pop open. Madra settled deeper into her chest, and she gave the pup a tender caress.

"Next stop, Vandalia," Kyle said.

Rita yawned. "I just had a worrying thought. What will we do with Madra while we eat?"

Vandalia

The usual early-May cold spell had not materialized, and the Accord's instrument panel said it was eighty-eight degrees outside. Rita kissed the top of Madra's head, and he blinked and stretched. He yawned, his tongue curling out of his mouth. He turned onto his back, and she would have sworn that he batted his eyes at her. She rubbed his belly, just as she did when he visited the store.

Kyle pulled off I-70 and drove half a block to the restaurant.

"They repainted it," he said. "It was natural wood the last time I was here."

The pristine white paint had to be new work, she thought. Maybe the place had gentrified. She hoped the meal would be what Kyle hoped for.

He circled the building, then parked by the front door.

"I was hoping for shade. I wonder if we can bring him in."

"I'll ask." She set Madra on the seat and ran through the blast of heat into the restaurant. A young woman in a navy polo shirt greeted her. "Quick question. It's too hot for our little dog. Can we bring him in?"

The server looked over her shoulder. "I'm not a hundred percent on that. All the owner can do is kick you out, right?"

"You'll give us to-go boxes if he does, yeah?"

"Yeah. Doggie bags." They both laughed. She ran back to the car and leashed Madra. Kyle turned off the car and grabbed Madra's bowl and some food. They took Madra for a quick walk, then stepped nonchalantly into the restaurant.

"Remodeled on the inside, too," Kyle said. Rita had not expected to see hanging flower baskets over every booth. The floor was laminate rather than old linoleum, and the medium-brown molding accented the white walls without closing in the space.

"Did it have a greasy-spoon vibe before?" she asked.

"Somewhat. Darker, very little contrast."

The server led them to the booth closest to the door. Kyle tucked Madra under the table and fed him. Rita asked for two coffees. The server, her long brown hair tied up and a smile on her face, brought two mugs that read "Chuck Wagon Café" and sported ads from local businesses. Each mug held a spoon in case they wanted milk or sugar.

Rita read the ads. "Is this a practical idea? I've seen place mats with ads for plumbers and real-estate agents before, but mugs? What do they do if one of their advertisers goes to prison or something?"

"There will be a big mug-smashing event, I suppose. Do you need cream or sugar?"

"My dad taught me to drink my coffee black."

"So did mine. I thought it was an Indiana thing, but you're from Detroit, right?"

"Good memory," Rita replied. "You're from Gary?"

"My dad's from Shoals, but he moved north before I was born."

Rita picked up the paper menu. "The menu reminds me of Shoals. Are you going to have frog legs, catfish, or bluegill?"

"It's a tough choice. I miss lake perch, but I love bluegill. What about you?"

"I'd say all-you-can-eat walleye, but if they throw us out because of Madra, it would be a waste."

"He can be very discreet." He nodded toward the far corner of the dining area. "Check out the Red Hat Society meeting." A dozen mature women were showing their liberation from societal norms by dressing in purple and wearing red hats.

Rita turned around. "Ha. They're cheating a bit. They aren't the rebels the poem calls for."

"What do you mean?" he asked.

"The poem is about a woman who plans to avoid aging gracefully. The red hat is supposed to not suit her. Half of these women are wearing Cardinals baseball caps, which surely suit them. Down here, a Cardinals cap is conformist."

"Would you join the Red Hat Society?"

"You have to be fifty to join. I'm only eligible to be a Pink Hatter now, and pink doesn't suit me. That makes me fit the poem, I suppose. Not that red is a good color for me." *And I won't live till fifty anyway,* she thought.

They ordered bluegill and looked at the route to St. Louis on Kyle's phone.

"We'll get there early. Do you want to go to the Arch? It's just a couple of miles off the freeway."

"Oh! The Gateway Arch. I haven't been. I've seen it when the Cardinals are on TV. It would be my first national park, too. I would love that." She would pack so many new experiences, so many memories, into this trip. "But let me know if you need to move west faster than we're going."

"I'm glad we have time together," he replied. "Have you noticed the family at that big table?" He pointed over her shoulder. She turned slowly. Four women and two men sat with a preteen boy who was in a motorized wheelchair. He had a huge smile on his face as he chatted with his family.

"This is my first time in a restaurant," he told the server. "I want to try frog legs."

Rita turned back to Kyle and caught him in a wistful gaze. "What a beautiful child," she said.

"He's what, maybe ten?" he whispered. "What a great attitude toward life."

The boy turned toward them. "Uncle Carl, is that a dog?" His bell-like voice rang through the restaurant. Kyle handed Rita the leash and walked over to their table. Rita looked at the servers. No sign that they cared about Madra.

"Do you like dogs?" Kyle asked the boy.

"I sure do!"

"Could I bring him over?" The adults all agreed. Rita clicked her tongue at Madra, who jumped to his feet. He trotted straight to the boy and placed his forepaws on the arm of the chair. The boy patted Madra and got his hand licked in return. He giggled.

"This is Madra," Kyle said.

"I'm Teddy." The adults turned out to be his grandparents, aunts, and an uncle. Rita pulled hand sanitizer from her purse and offered it to Teddy. He held out his hand, and while he rubbed it into his palms, she noticed that the women at the table looked relieved. She paid the tab and led Madra back into the blazing afternoon. Kyle followed a moment later.

"If I don't ever have kids," he said, "I would want to adopt a special-needs child like him. He has such a beautiful soul."

She thought she saw tears welling in his eyes, and without thinking, she hugged him for the first time. She feared she wouldn't get to hug him often enough before she left him behind.

1941, London
by Colleen Haggerty

Julia felt pulled in many directions. On the one hand, she had
a two-year-old toddler. In their small flat, Will was getting
into everything. Not that there was much to get into. Julia had
sold everything she could, just to have money for food. But
anything Will could get his hands on, he did. He pulled towels
off the rack in the water closet, found the pots and pans in the
cupboard and banged them together like he was in a band, and
took her dirty clothes from the hamper and wore them, pranc-
ing around the flat like he was a pretty lady. Adorable as he
was, he was a handful.

On the other hand, she had her mother living about a mile
away with a parade of aches and pains marching through her
life now that she was older. Her mum had always been an independent woman, had been ever since she lost her husband
in the Great War. Julia didn't know a lot about his death except that he died in a trench in Northern France. With help
from her parents, her mum raised Julia on her own.

Julia begged her mother to move in with her and Will, but she refused. Her mother was fierce about staying in her own flat "until they take me out feet first." Between Will, her mother, making ends meet, and worrying about when the next bomb would drop—and where—Julia was exhausted.

It didn't matter what time Will went to bed; Julia could never get a good night's sleep. She flopped like a beached fish thinking about Jimmy, her husband. Each night she went through a litany of scenarios. She imagined him in a tent in a field in whichever country his last letter had come from. She imagined him at the mess hall hunched over a plate of canned meat, scarfing the food down trying to satiate his hunger. She imagined him sitting on his cot, a flashlight in his mouth illuminating his lap as he wrote her a letter. She worried about him, so much. She couldn't allow space for the other images, but they woke her up anyway, unbidden. Those came when she was finally in a deep sleep: Jimmy running from a trench on a mission right into enemy fire. A bullet piercing the air and then Jimmy's heart. Jimmy's chest caving in as his body was thrust back into the trench. Jimmy's body slamming into the far side of the trench, blood spilling out of his body like a river. Each night she woke with a start, a gasp, and sweat framing her face. Each night she could hardly breathe as she oriented herself to her room, the clock on her bedside table, the picture of her and Jimmy on their wedding day in a simple silver frame atop the dresser, Will's crib on the far side of her bed. Each night she waited for her breathing to slow down, until she could hear Will's breath, shallow and sure.

Sometimes Julia couldn't get back to sleep. She kept Jimmy's letters in the bedside drawer for such occasions. That's when she would take one out and re-read it. They all opened with the same sentiment, "Julia, I miss you so much I could break." She could almost hear his voice cracking. Sometimes he wrote about the war, but mostly he talked about his mates and their antics. He signed each letter the same way, "Yours always. Jimmy." Always is a long time. She had to believe he was coming home. There was no other way to exist. Those terrifying dreams were her mind's way of playing tricks on her. Julia prided herself on being chipper. These dreams shook her to the core for they were so unlike her nature.

It didn't help that in each of Jimmy's letters there was something unsaid, something big and alive and as terrifying as her dreams. She didn't know what, really. She didn't even know if Jimmy knew. They didn't know how to do this except to just get through each day.

On those extra difficult nights after a dream, Julia finished the letter, kissed it softly, returned it to its envelope and shut out the light. She followed her baby's breath into slumber.

Being exhausted wasn't the only reason Julia had a hard time managing. Julia's mother was getting older and more frail. Prone to influenza, as well as frequent nasty colds, whenever her mum had something contagious, Julia always left Will with her neighbor Muriel so he wouldn't catch anything. And that's just what she did that night.

After she fed Will an early dinner, Julia pushed aside her regular kitchen curtain with yellow and lavender flowers and the blackout curtains behind them. How she hated those curtains, how she hated the need for them. Damn Jerrys. She had to find a clear spot in the window to look through. Tape was adhered to each window in various X formations. While this ensured that glass shards wouldn't fly into the room should a bomb shatter the window, it was like looking through a window smeared with petroleum jelly.

She looked out the window between the tape to a sky that was cloudy, giving the sunset an eerie orange glow. *No bomber moon tonight.* No matter, she still grabbed Will's siren suit and stuffed it in the overnight bag. "Come now, Will, time to go to Muriel's. You lucky boy, you get another sleepover with her again. Will you be playing with the puppets?" Will loved the donkey and sheep puppets at Muriel's, puppets Muriel bought when Will was about a year old and started spending the night with her so Julia could tend to her mother. Julia didn't dare sneak back home after curfew.

Julia grabbed Will's pudgy little hand and walked him across the hallway to Muriel's flat.

Muriel opened the door, "Hello, sweet William. How's my boy today?"

Will ran up to Muriel and grabbed the hem of her flowered house dress. "Muwiwo!"

Muriel laughed. "That never gets old, does it? Has he had supper?" she asked as Julia dropped a bag of diapers and pajamas inside the doorway.

"Yes. Thanks so much for helping out again, Muriel. You're a peach." Julia bent to give Muriel a swift kiss on the cheek. Julia didn't know how she would have survived the war without Muriel. Friends since secondary school, it was Muriel who introduced her to Jimmy. Julia laughed at herself now for how jealous she was when she was first getting to know Jimmy. They were so chummy, she assumed Muriel and Jimmy were dating. In fact, they were more like siblings. They had known each other since they were babes-in-arms;

their mums knew each other since they were pregnant. This meant Muriel was like Will's auntie.

"Always my pleasure, Julia," she said as she picked up Will and hiked him to her hip. Will giggled as she tickled his side. Julia nuzzled her nose into Will's neck and gave him a raspberry on the soft spot under his ear. Her heart ached to see Muriel so attentive to Will, knowing that Muriel had lost her own late in pregnancy just three years before. *I hope her Andrew gets home from the war soon so they can try again*, Julia thought. Julia felt an excitement flutter in her womb at the thought of babies. Her desire, the things people don't talk about in wartime, was to have Jimmy come home safe and sound, to get pregnant again and have two more children.

"Mommy will see you in the morning, sweet pea. I love my little Will." Julia looked at Muriel. "It doesn't look like a bomber's moon tonight, too cloudy. I think we're safe, but his siren suit is in the bag, just in case. I know it's a little big for him, but there's such a small chance you'll need it."

"Julia. Don't worry. We've been over this a million times. When has there ever been a bomb when you spent the night with your mum? It'll be fine." Muriel put her hand on Julia's arm and gave a pat.

Will leaned into Julia's face, "Bye, bye, Mama," and tried to return the raspberry, but his inexperience left a running slurp of saliva down her check. Julia and Muriel laughed as Julia wiped the spit from her face. She turned and walked out the door.

The walk to her mother's house took Julia about ten minutes, less if she walked quickly. But walking quickly scared Julia, like she was running from something. She didn't want to feel scared, so she defiantly took her time, setting a gentle, civilized pace. There weren't many people out at this time, it being almost curfew. She knew she could make it by dark. The hazy orange sky she saw earlier gave way to a brighter orange. Where clouds hung from the sky just twenty minutes ago, now she could see a few early evening stars. Julia felt a prick of fear in her neck. *Don't be silly*, she thought, *there won't be any bombs tonight.* The fear wasn't listening and instead sat heavy in her gut.

By the time she arrived at her mum's flat, the clouds had risen and floated away. She considered turning right back around, going back to Will, but if she did that, she felt like the Germans would be controlling her, manipulating her. Her mother was ill and needed her. Will was fine, probably playing with the puppets at that very moment. She walked up to her mother's flat and inserted the key into the front door.

"Hello Mum," Julia said loudly, knowing her mum was likely in the bedroom. "Mum?" Julia beelined it to her mother's room to see how she was doing. As she approached, she could hear her mother's loud purring. That's what Julia called it. Her mum didn't snore, she purred, like a loud cat. Maybe this is what lions sound like. As a child, Julia was always an early riser. As a young girl she would scamper into her mum's bedroom, ready to start the day, and her mum would always be purring. Hearing that sound from her mother that night flooded Julia with a sense of security, belonging, and comfort.

Since her mum was sleeping, Julia made a U-turn and went to the kitchen. She put the teakettle on the stove and prepared the tea. From inside her bag, Julia pulled a chunk of cooked fish, the other half of which she had eaten earlier that day. She reached for the margarine on the shelf and scooped out a spoonful and scraped it into the frying pan, standing ready at the stovetop. Julia pulled out a bag of cut potatoes from her bag and tossed them into the frying pan, cooking them up to go with the cooked fish.

"Julia, is that you?" Julia's heart flinched when she heard her mother's feeble voice. *How did she get so old? What will it be like when I'm that old? Will my son feel the same pang in his heart?*

"Yes, Mum, just cooking up some chips and making tea. You hungry?"

"A little. Thank you, love."

When the food was warm and the tea had steeped, Julia brought them to her mother on a wooden tray. She set the tray on the dresser so she could help her mum sit up and eat. She ran her hands over her mother's forehead. Hot. Probably a hundred and one. "You think you can eat something, Mum?"

"I think so. Thank you for coming, Julia. How's Will today?"

Laying her angst aside, Julia picked up the tray from the dresser and set it over her mother's lap. "Oh, he's just fine. You should have seen him; he had on Jimmy's dress shoes and was stomping all over the flat pointing at things like he was a big man. I couldn't stop laughing, Mum."

Her mother laughed weakly. Julia poured the tea, black since there wasn't any milk or sugar to be had and set a napkin in her mother's lap. "Here you go, Mum."

Julia went to the bathroom, found a washcloth and soaked it in cold tap water. "Mum, you're feeling hot. Let's have you put this on your neck." She wrapped the wet cloth around the back of her mother's neck.

"Oh, that feels good. Thank you." Her mother sank back down into the bed.

"Mum, you need to eat something. At least have a few bites of the fish." Her mother straightened up and managed to eat some of the fish and a few chips. She sipped on her tea slowly.

"Do you want me to read to you? We've still got quite a way to go in *How Green Was My Valley.*"

"Maybe just a few pages, love. I'm pretty sleepy."

Julia picked up the tray and took it to the kitchen. She came back with a new washcloth, cold with water and, after removing the other, wrapped this one around her mum's neck. Julia sat in an overstuffed chair by her mother's bed, curled her feet under her and opened the book to the dog-eared page.

After five pages of reading, Julia was getting tired herself, so she was relieved when her mother started purring again. Julia turned down the corner of the page where she had finished reading, put the book on the bedside table and went to the kitchen to wash the dishes.

When she was done, she took the pile of sheets and blankets from the hall closet, the ones she used every time she spent the night here. She put the sheets on the brown sofa and then covered the top sheet with two blankets. After brushing her teeth, Julia walked to the living room window. Pushing the curtain and blackout curtain aside a few inches, she peeked outside. What she saw made her shiver from the inside out. The sky was perfectly clear, a bomber's moon. That could only mean one thing.

She knew it was against the rules, but she couldn't help herself, she just had to see, so she unclasped the window and pushed it open a few inches. The air was crisp and fresh. As she took in a deep breath, she scanned the horizon. She didn't see it at first, not until she looked directly overhead. A white parachute, about fifteen feet in diameter, was floating down from forty feet in the air. The night was suddenly silent. Julia looked around and didn't see any other parachutes, just this one. Hanging from the ropes attached to the parachute, Julia was sure there was a Jerry rigged in. She knew the Germans tried to ambush the British by sending down soldiers to kill people. Her heart clenched, both in hatred and fear. The parachute kept floating slowly down, coming closer to her window. As it drew nearer, it became clear that it wasn't a Jerry hanging from the parachute, but a bomb. A real, live bomb, coming her direction. Grey with a distinctive white band near the nose, which was pointing menacingly right toward her.

The air was perfectly still and silent. The parachute, taut from the weight of the bomb, looked so pure compared to the destructive filth hanging below. It continued to float silently toward her. *This is it, then. This is when I die.* She desperately wanted to run, fetch her mum and get back to Will, but her feet were like lead and stuck to the floor. She couldn't take her eyes off the parachute. *I'm about to die.*

When she had gone into labor with Will, she had been taken off guard by how quickly she progressed. Her labor was fast and intense. That was the only other time in her life when she thought she was going to die. The pain was so focused and sharp, she honestly didn't think she would survive. But she was luckier then than she would be tonight.

Julia took a deep breath and thought of Jimmy. *I never thought it would be* me *who died first.*

She thought of Jimmy getting word of her death, afraid that he might actually break in two. Months after she'd realized that Muriel and Jimmy weren't dating, after she and Jimmy had been flirting with each other through sideways glances and accidental brushes against each other, Jimmy took her out on a date. They had taken a walk and then stopped for tea and cake. While they were eating, he held her hand, caressing the back of it with his thumb. She had never felt her body tingle like that before and she hadn't wanted it to end. Her breath had become shallow and she'd felt like her heart was dripping inside her chest. They couldn't take their eyes off each other.

Yes, I think he'll actually break in two.

Julia heard a *whoosh*. Startled, she looked behind her for the sound and then realized that the sound was a gust of wind announcing itself outside the window. That simple burst of air slung the parachute away, the bomb swinging in the air below like a clock pendulum. She stood, transfixed on the retreating bomb as it floated further and further away, closer and closer to the Earth.

The parachute ultimately floated blocks away. Even from where she stood, she could hear the bomb land with a metal *thunk* on a brick bomb shelter. The explosion was nearly deafening, nearly blinding. She shielded her eyes from the bright fire.

"Julia! Julia! What's happening?" Her mother's voice wasn't nearly as loud as she'd likely intended; Julia could tell she didn't have the strength to yell.

"It's all right, Mum. It's all right." Julia still couldn't move. Couldn't close the window. Couldn't take her eyes off the fire, now that the initial brightness had worn off. Sirens wailed and the sounds of commotion started up. She imagined the white parachute burning into black ash.

"Julia! What happened? Was it a bomb?" Her mother stood at the doorway between her bedroom and the living room. Julia quickly shut and latched the window, pulled the curtains tight and scurried over to her mother.

The phosphorus smell from the bomb had wafted over to where they stood hugging each other. "I saw the whole thing, Mum, I saw it all." She couldn't manage to tell her mother that the bomb had been coming right toward them. She couldn't admit that she was so shocked by the whole ordeal that she did nothing to protect her mother from impending death.

As Julia helped her mother back to bed, her mother tried to comfort Julia. "Oh, love, I'm so sorry. That must have been awful."

"Mum! Will. I have to go see if Will is okay!" She looked around the flat making sure everything was safe for her to leave. "Are you okay if I don't stay..."

"Julia. Go. Now. I'm fine." Her mother whooshed her away with her wrinkled hands. "Go."

"Thanks Mum." Julia grabbed her coat and bag. "I'll check in with you tomorrow."

What took her ten minutes to walk when she was defiantly cocky took her only five minutes to run as a worried mother. She was out of breath by the time she was pounding on Muriel's door. "Muriel! Muriel!" As the door cracked open, Julia pushed it with her body, sprinting to Muriel's bedroom where she knew Will always slept. At the threshold, she stopped short, saw her little boy curled around the donkey puppet, thumb in his mouth. Julia slumped to her knees and wept.

She didn't even notice Muriel rubbing her back. "It's okay, Julia. He's okay." She kept rubbing Julia's back as it heaved with relief and sorrow. Julia couldn't help but think of the toddlers in the shelter whose bodies were blown to bits. The mothers who were killed. And there was her boy, lying on the bed, sucking his thumb, holding a donkey. The two women huddled on the floor in a heap of tears.

Tonight the women and child had survived. Julia said a silent prayer that their men had been so lucky.

The Kind of People Who Leave Dirt on the Floor
by Alyson Indrunas

One day when I was a little girl, no more than ten, riding in the car with my dad on our way to a campground, I told him I wanted to be a hairdresser when I grew up. He cut me off before I could even explain how much I loved being at the hair salon, before I could tell him how glamorous I thought it would be to work with other women all day, before I could say why I thought hairdressers were having fun in their jobs.

"No. You don't," he snapped.

He turned to look at me while he was driving. I didn't meet his eyes. I looked out the window and felt my soul flying away.

"You want to do something with your brain." He sounded so serious. "Why would you want to spend your time with a bunch of gossiping women. C'mon." The disappointment dripped through his words. "That's bullshit. What else do you want to be, kid? Think." Now he sounded pissed off.

I stared at the profile of his angry face.

I'd always struggled to figure out what adults were really thinking. They were such a mystery to me. They knew something I did not and I couldn't wait to understand.

This was a man who routinely confused me by telling me *don't throw like a girl* or *eat onions, they'll put hair on your chest.* I'd contort my head the way a dog does when it hears an odd sound. Was throwing like a girl bad? I hated onions. And why should I care about hair on my chest? He clearly knew how to talk to a son but was confused by what to say to a daughter. "Well, I guess I have a cheerleader instead of a football player" is what he said when I was born.

Sitting in the car that day, I gave it more thought: *What did I want to be?* My little brain spun. I had just watched the movie *Legal Eagles,* and I thought about the love story between Debra Winger and Robert Redford that blossomed during the exciting court drama.

"I'd like to be a lawyer," I said. My dad smiled. I had no idea what it meant to be a lawyer but based on that movie, it looked like it would help me attract men from a bygone era who liked women in business suits.

At that time, I had never seen a woman in a business suit; seeing Debra Winger in one stunned me. I had seen women in their Sunday finest church dresses, but not a proper business suit, carrying a briefcase. Winger's character wore her suit like a uniform. All the women I knew wore the aprons of early-morning grocery-bakers or those of house cleaners. Women I knew worked nine-to-five jobs that they hated. Debra Winger's character not only had a cool job, she had snagged the Sundance Kid. Hot damn. Being a lawyer looked great.

My dad looked pleased that I went from attending beauty school to studying for the LSAT in less than ten minutes. He praised me with a "Good kid" expression and, like a great dad, he kept it to himself if he had any doubts that I could ever follow a lawyer's path. He nodded as if I was a girl who was destined to go to college, to law school, no less. He nodded as if I wouldn't be the next woman in the family who wore an apron to work every day.

But that question of what I really wanted to be: It never left me.

I carried that question for years. It sat on my chest throughout my teenage years, and then it parked itself in my heart as my twenties loomed around the corner. I couldn't think of any answer that felt quite right.

Until the summer I worked at Yellowstone National Park when I was nineteen years old.

The Welcome Center at the park was a crossroads where people from all over the world stopped to rest and spend some time indoors. These tourists bought souvenirs and gathered information from rangers. I loved my daily errand to the Welcome Center, not only to mail letters or postcards to my friends, but also so I could be around the travelers from exotic places. The Welcome Center was also a much-needed break from the relentless interactions of employee dorm life where nothing was private. Having been an only child, I was unaccustomed to sharing my living space with other people. All that time in a building with strangers, including very attractive boys from California, was overwhelming at times. The Welcome Center was a wonderful respite and a great place to people watch.

One day when I walked into the tourist Welcome Center, I was wearing my park-issued kitchen apron—a sous-chef after her shift. I couldn't take my eyes off a group of employees huddled together near the massive fireplace. I was amazed at all the gear they had.

One man, who was impossibly fit with arms as beefy as a football player's, walked around taking inventory of sleeping bags and mats, cooking pots and food. Another woman with equally sculpted arms, was counting tents and tent stakes. The others were chatting and joking around with each other while they were packing things into small plastic bags like first aid supplies and trail mix. They seemed excited to be getting ready to go to work. *Who are these people? Where are they going? How do you get that job?*

I came to learn that they were the trail crew. It had never occurred to me that some people worked outside in nature all day. Nor did I have any idea that people could be happy with the work they were doing. It was a cosmic boom in the universe for me. *Getting paid for something that you enjoy?*

On the day I saw my first trail crew, it was love at first sight.

I asked the cashier at the Welcome Center, a woman from Illinois who lived on the same floor as me, about them. Without a beat, she rolled her eyes and spat, "Fucking trail crew, man. I always have to sweep twice after they leave because they get dirt and peanuts everywhere. You know what fucking maniacs management can be about food on the floor. Don't people come to Yellowstone to see the wildlife? Surely they can enjoy a fucking field mouse eating up the shit these hippie fuckers leave on the floor."

Just then we watched two trail crew dudes spill half a pack of M&Ms and peanuts on the floor. My dorm mate exhaled loudly.

"They say there aren't any wolves in Yellowstone. They haven't seen how these fuckers live. So gross. The kind of people that leave dirt on the floor." She shook her head slowly.

For every ounce of rage and contempt she felt for them, I was suddenly filled with an equal amount of love. I noticed they were wearing the same ridiculous name tags all Yellowstone employees were required to wear one inch above our hearts: Your name and your home state in large letters next to the logo of Old Faithful. I spent the entire summer explaining to people that my last name was not Georgia. I would count to three and then listen to them say how shocked they were that I didn't have a southern accent (I lived in Atlanta). I'd then suffer through some anecdote about Jimmy Carter (fans or critics), *Gone with the Wind* (yes, I had been to Margaret Mitchell's house), or Ted Turner (can you believe he's dating Hanoi Jane).

I politely smiled through these conversations with The Tourons, as we affectionately called them, because a mere complaint from them could get us fired by our managers, who wore blue pins with white letters and black pants and white shirts. Listening to The Tourons say stupid banal shit was just part of the job. Your only duty was to tell them not to go near the bison or the elk.

As part of the onboarding process of my job, they made me watch a video where a very short man with a telephoto lens walks closer and closer to a bison. Just as the man settles in to take the shot, the bison charges him, head down towards his chest, and with the flick of its massive neck, sends the man sailing into the air.

The narrator says, "It is your duty to remind the tourists of the danger of wild animals." The tape ended. I waited for about two seconds and started a full belly laugh. *Why didn't he just use the telephoto lens?* I thought.

I watched as the trail crew shared jokes with each other in their small group and ignored the patrons milling around the welcome center. Smiling. It seemed to me like they found a way to escape living among The Tourons. I had discovered that once I hiked three miles away from any trailhead, I lost eighty percent of the Touron population. The people I did see that far out were people I would want to meet. I did a test once with a small group I met in the backcountry: I mentioned Ted Turner dating Jane Fonda. Without a beat, one of them quoted *Barbarella* and another shared how much they loved her in *Barefoot in the Park*. Didn't say a word about Ted Turner.

Yes, the trail crew headed into the woods every day and got paid for it. This totally blew my mind.

My People.

I observed the mud on their boots, their strong arms, their tans.

I sighed and thought about the list of jobs on the Yellowstone application, the ones that required a college degree or Wilderness First Aid training. I didn't check those boxes when I applied for this summer job. I stuck to the jobs where you had to wear an apron.

I turned to the cashier, Ashley, Illinois, and asked, "What do they do out there?"

"They fix the trails and shit and load up their boots with mud to leave it all over my floor. When they aren't making a mess on my fucking floor, they're cutting down trees that block the trails. Then they must eat all the food that they haven't spilled on the floor around the fireplace. Fucking hippy pigs."

We watched a guy shovel a handful of sunflower seeds into his mouth and a third of them fell on the floor. He shoveled more into his mouth and didn't bother picking up what he had dropped.

"For fuck's sake," Ashley, Illinois, said, rolling her eyes.

I knew I wasn't going to get a good answer from her, so I took a seat on the government issue couch by the fireplace. I watched one of the girls use her bandana to wipe the sweat from her hairy armpit, and then she rolled it up to pull back her hair. Genius!

This group of people, the trail crew, cracked open a whole new world for me. I watched them put on their packs and file out the door one by one with their eyes on the mountains ahead.

I wasn't sure what my dad or the rest of my family would think of me spending my life on a trail, but that, I decided right then and there, was living.

Something to Remember Me By
by Anneliese Kamola

The Texan sun baked the black asphalt to white. I sat in the backseat of my Auntie Angela's cream Chevrolet Astro minivan as she drove me and my grandmother—my Oma—to a big box store. One of those Texas-sized big box stores which was about twice as big as anything I was used to in Washington State. I looked through the windshield and saw ribbons of heatwaves rippling over the road.

Oma lived with my dad's sister, Angela, her husband, Steve, and their kids, Stephanie and Bennett, in Houston, Texas. We had all mourned my Opa's death from cancer several years earlier, but now at close to a hundred years old, my Oma was still kickin'. She only took a daily multivitamin. She pushed her walker on long, glacially slow walks down the driveway to the mailbox. On her way back, she'd stop and sit on her walker's built-in seat and gaze up at the towering pecan trees lining the drive.

Once home to her mother-in-law suite, Oma would lay down on a low bed in the screened-in front porch and take a nap. She slept a lot. I spent much of my days sitting in a chair next to her bed, soaking up my time with her—she couldn't last forever. I watched the dappled light dance across her tan skin and took in the shape of her face, her defined cheekbones, the notch to the bridge of her nose, and how her gray-white hair seemed to float over her forehead.

Oma fascinated me. She had straight posture which still struck me as upright even as she started to hunch with age. She was somehow regal, even lying on a porch bed. She always wore pearl necklaces and clip-on gold earrings, her cuticles were always cut back, and she wore bright lipstick. She was a different kind of grandma. A no-nonsense kind of grandma, as opposed to my mom's mom, my Grandma Betty, who "went about with her tails a-flappin!" as she said, meaning her shirt untucked. Grandma Betty felt like a playmate, wearing long necklaces with pendants from around the world. She was cozy and funny, gregarious and easy to know. But Oma carried her Austrian heritage with her, even into elderhood.

Sometimes when Oma woke from her nap, she'd hook her pointer finger toward me. I'd get up and sit down next to her on the bed, and she'd take my hand in both of hers. We'd sit there like that, in silence, watching the pecan leaves glitter. I wondered if she felt lonely, or if she was content, or a mixture of both, but I never had the courage to ask. Time felt expansive when I sat next to her, and when I matched my breathing with hers, I felt slow was the perfect way to live.

Sometimes I asked her questions about her life: she grew up in Alexandria, Egypt, the daughter of a famous Austrian painter. WWI forced her family to return to Europe, and they settled in Germany. Oma became a German *Fraulein*. She grew up to own a small weaving factory in Dachau, Germany, and to be a family friend with Rudolf Hess, the third in command of Germany under Hitler in the early years of WWII. As time went on, Oma used concentration camp prisoners in her factory. She became friends with them and her political perspective changed. At the end of the war she risked her life to break some of the men out of Dachau—including my future Opa, a Polish Army officer and prisoner of war.

She was courageous, yet she always seemed a little sad. When I asked about her life, Oma would reply about the facts of her life—who, what, where, when. I sometimes asked about how she felt about things, and she said, "Read my autobiography. Everything is in there." I had read it; she hadn't written much about her feelings. I didn't realize then, but I was hungry to know the vulnerable parts to her—who she was and *why* she was and, therefore, who and why I was, too.

Once, instead of answering questions, she inspected my hand. "Oh, *meine kleine Kartoffelin*," she said, using her pet name for me, her Little Potato. "These two fingernails," she stroked my left pinky and ring fingers, "look like mine. The rest must have come from your Grandma Betty." It was true; she and I shared long, deep, left hand pinkie and ring nails. My other nails were rounder, like my mom's, my grandma's, even my great-grandma's on my maternal side. That was a nice thought—I carried the women of my family in my hands.

"Anneliese," Oma had said to me just that morning. "I want to buy you something on this trip. Something to remember me by. So you will remember to live a good life. Perhaps something special from Texas?"

This was the first time she had mentioned her mortality to me. It scared me a bit. But, ever the good granddaughter, I obliged her wishes to leave me a tangible gift as a legacy. As incongruous as it felt, there was only one thing I really wanted from Texas: a pair of cowboy boots. I could get boots up in Washington State, but they wouldn't be *authentic*.

I had wanted cowboy boots ever since I was a little girl. My dad wore smooth, shiny, honey- and molasses-toned boots as dress shoes. I loved watching him hook his pointer fingers through the loops on either side of his right boot's upper. He'd slip his foot in and, with a tug, pull the boot up around his foot, as if with a pop. Then he'd do it again with the left. He'd stand and walk across the linoleum front hall, his footsteps crisp clicks. And later, when I sat between him and Mom in the Auburn Performing Arts Center, if I listened close enough, I could hear his boot *tap tap tap* on the cement floor as he kept time with the music.

As the years went on, my love for boots expanded to the movies. In late middle school, Mom, Dad, and I got on a kick of watching old black and white Spaghetti Western movies on Friday nights. I liked watching Gary Cooper, Steve McQueen, and Clint Eastwood in their dust-covered cowboy boots, calm, standing stalwart in a street shoot-out. I was entering puberty and my emotions were starting to heat up. I longed to stand with aplomb.

And then, somewhere in early high school, I saw a woman in her late twenties wearing black cowboy boots with a pretty summer dress at a party. Those boots mixed creativity with confidence into a new aesthetic of feminine beauty. Something in this gal's gait caught my attention. She walked differently in those boots. Her pelvis dropped lower toward the ground. Her body spoke with "sassitude," saying, without words, *I'm in charge, I'm a powerhouse, don't mess with me.* Good Lord, I wanted to walk like that.

So, when my Oma asked what I wanted from Texas, my college-aged-self pulled out my childhood dreams of cowboy boots. Here was my opportunity—originality, calm, and power!

"Thank you, Oma," I said. "You know, I'd like a pair of cowboy boots, please."

"You want to remember me with cowboy boots?" she asked, raising her eyebrows.

I couldn't help but grin. "I'll remember you anyhow but, yes, cowboy boots."

She just shrugged her shoulders and nodded, and later at lunch told my aunt we needed to go shopping that afternoon for boots.

When told, Angela raised her eyebrows toward me in response to her mother's bossy ways. I loved my Aunt Angela. She was impossibly kind. She always said, "Yes, Ma'am," and, "No, Sir," even to the neighbors. She was tall, blonde, and stylish—she could somehow make wearing two different colors of denim at the same time look good. As a kid, I'd wanted to be *just* as tall and pretty as her when I grew up; she was a *babe.* She looked at me now and smiled, ever the gracious host.

"Yes, Ma'am."

I smiled back. I was excited about the boots, of course. But I felt a tinge of sorrow, too. Oma had never mentioned her death before. How could this legend die? She had always been there, a backbone, a force of respect and propriety.

But soon my thoughts of my boots crawled over my looming sorrow, and I started to scheme. Brown boots? Blonde? Black? Red? Mmmmm—definitely red. Calf-high? Anklets? Gotta be calf high—more supportive. Chunky? Narrow? Well, these weren't boots just for fashion; they had to be serviceable, so whatever felt the best. Overlapping leather tooled design, or a single leather piece with stitching? Whatever looked best. And definitely bootstraps. I didn't want zippers, ease, or cheating to get them on. I needed those loops, just like my dad had on his. My boots had to be classic, bold, with a splash of character.

After forty minutes or so of driving, Angela turned the minivan left into the parking lot of *Boot Town USA*. My breath caught as, after we parked, I opened the backseat door and the heat blasted me like I'd hit a wall. I never could get used to the heat and bright, bright sunlight of Texas. I opened Oma's door and helped her out of the front seat and into the wheelchair, which Angela had brought from the back of the van. Oma wore black wrap-around sunglasses and white Velcro shoes, incongruous with her name-brand jacket and golden necklace. The two of us settled her in, and Angela pulled her back while I locked and closed the doors.

We crossed the parking lot toward the store. The sliding glass front doors opened with a whoosh, and we stepped through a downdraft of forced icy air. Before my eyes could adjust to the fluorescent lights, I smelled leather and cardboard. A twangy country song played. After a moment I could see a labyrinth of shelves—towers of boxes and possibilities. Somewhere in this Texas-sized store had to be a pair of sassy, sexy, red, calf-high, sturdy yet elegant boots made just for me. Boots that would keep my feet tapping to a beat, and boost both my poise and my sex appeal.

We set out to find them. Angela rolled Oma down the wide aisles. I watched as they picked up and inspected boots. Oma was blind in one eye, so she held each boot really close to her face. I noticed both Angela's and Oma's profiles were like mine—that of a sharp-eyed hawk. Perhaps, together, we would see just the right pair.

"Here, try this on," Angela said, handing me a pair of black boots. With a thrill of anticipation, I slid my feet in and tried walking down the aisle.

"My feet are slipping around," I said to my auntie, handing the boots back to her. She nodded.

"Okay, try this one," she said, taking the tan boot from Oma and handing it to me. I tried that one on, too, but shook my head.

"This one pinches my toes."

I tried on a dozen pairs of boots. Every time, walking down the row, seeking the gait with which I had seen other booted women walk, my feet just felt squashed, or pinched, or sloshy and sliding. Was this what cowboy boots really felt like? Had I been deluding myself all these years? Or were Angela and Oma just not finding the right ones? I felt anything but competent as I wobbled around.

After a few minutes, frustration knotting in my belly, I went off on my own. And then I saw them. Red. Beautiful red boots, with multicolored flowers embroidered down the sides. They were perfect and everything I had dreamed of. But then I noticed the price tag: $347.00. Holy cow, that was too much! I couldn't ask Oma to buy me boots that expensive. Looking around, though, the boots in the price range I was anticipating Oma to be comfortable with, around $60.00, were all flimsy and short, with thin, synthetic leather and, worst of all, *zippers*.

I was about to give up. Everything I had dreamed of was out of my assumed price range. I could just walk back to Oma and say, "Never mind, I was mistaken, boots aren't for me, just get me a purse instead." But I imagined her looking at me, raising her eyebrow, shocked.

"Anneliese," she would probably say, "You do not stand firm in your decision?"

I wanted to be composed and courageous, like her. I was the granddaughter of guts, of class, of perseverance. Okay. I would find a pair I loved that wouldn't break Oma's bank no matter how long I had to look. In a snap tactical maneuver, I decided to let go of my desire for red. Surely, I could find *one* authentic, well-made pair of boots for a reasonable price in this big store.

Just then, a pair of boots on a top shelf caught my eye. Caramel-brown cowhide. Classic, simple, with cream-colored stitching of a thistle pattern. The toes pointed upward ever so slightly. The heels were thick and sturdy. And attached to the V-dip on the top edge of the upper were perfect bootstrap loops. They were $99.00.

I traced my finger down the stack of boxes below the demo pair, found my size, and pulled out the box. I opened the lid, then lifted the boots out one at a time. I noted how the leather felt stiff under my hands yet still somehow soft. I kicked off my sandals and sat down on the cement floor. Hooking my middle fingers into the bootstraps, I angled my foot into the upper and, in a single, smooth motion, slid my toes in as far as the heel. I pulled the bootstraps with a little extra force and my foot popped into place. The arch was in just the right spot. The boot formed right around the toes. I stood and walked down the aisle. I didn't wobble and I wasn't in any pain. I felt how the heel pushed my body's pressure forward onto the balls of my feet, into a physical stance that made me feel ready for action. And yet I could also rest back onto the strong, sturdy heels, rocking my hips down and forward. These shoes would hold all of me. I felt my body adjust to a new stance of power. I felt sexy and strong, like I could go out and kick some ass. They were perfect.

Grinning like a fool, I picked up the box and my sandals and went to find Oma and Angela.

"I think I found them," I said. I turned my feet right, then left. I walked down the aisle and back, modeling my posture and newly forming gait.

Oma tilted her head to her right and looked at my feet. Had I chosen okay? Would she scold me for something too elaborate?

"Yes, we get them," she said with her slight German accent, a note of finality in her voice. "They look good."

I beamed.

Oma motioned for me to give her the box and my sandals, which she tucked inside the cardboard amidst the tissue paper. She closed the lid.

Angela pushed Oma to the front counter, and I walked beside them. I heard my boots *tap tap tap* on the linoleum— light, crisp. I stood tall as the three of us women chatted with the cashier.

"You enjoy those now, Miss," said the lady behind the counter as she looked at my boots. "They look real nice on you."

"Yes, Ma'am," I replied. "Thank you."

As Oma slipped her debit card back into her beige purse, I bent over and kissed her cheek.

"Thank you, Oma. This is a perfect gift." She tilted her head back to look at me. Her eyes were big and brown. She smiled and tapped my cheek with her hand. "Now you will remember me."

"Always."

As we left the store, I felt the heat of the Houston summer sun on my cheeks. I squinted my eyes, more with sass than against the glare. And it was with calm, pelvis-tucked confidence that I pushed Oma's wheelchair to the minivan.

The night before Halloween, two years later, I turned off the last light and opened the front door of the house I was renting with college friends. They had all gone out already; I had stayed behind to finish the last touches on a paper for my creative writing class. I was wearing a dress and, of course, my cowboy boots. I held a bottle of Jack Daniels; I had to shift it to the other hand to pull my ringing cell phone from my coat pocket. I flipped it open with my thumb.

"Hello?"

"Anneliese? It's your dad."

What was he doing calling? He never called; he usually emailed. "Hey Dad, you just caught me, I was on my way out. What's up?" I asked, closing the door and walking back into the living room, the sunset through the picture window lighting my way.

There was a pause on the other end of the line.

"Your Oma died this evening."

The air went out of my lungs. I set the Jack Daniels down on the side table and crossed to the window to look out at the bay. My eyes traced over the islands to the tangerine sky. I gently placed the tips of my fingers against the glass and nodded.

"Oh." I didn't have anything to say. Of course, we knew her death was coming—she was a hundred and one after all—but now that it was here I felt only stillness inside my body. "Okay." There was a long pause which no words needed to fill. "Thanks for telling me. You alright?"

"Yeah, I am. I will be," he said. I nodded, even though he couldn't see me. "You?"

"I'm not sure yet," I said, "But I'm sure I will be."

"Call tomorrow if you want," he said.

"Yeah, okay. I will. Bye Dad, thanks again." We hung up. I returned the phone to my pocket.

Everything was quiet, just as it had been when I sat next to her on the porch in Texas. I just stood in the dark room looking out the window. My Oma, my grandmother of power and dignity, of opinion, judgment, tenacity. Gone. And then, as if catching up with my shock, grief knotted my belly, and I started to cry so hard I almost threw up. I dropped onto the futon and cried and cried, feeling the finality of everything. Never again would I get to curl up next to her on long summer days. Never again would I feel her cool hand pat my cheek. Never again would I get to ask questions and hear her stories. I slid my left thumb along my left pinkie, from nail to second knuckle, my finger narrow and straight, just like hers. Every now and then I looked up to see the sunset blurred through tears.

After twenty minutes or so the tears settled. My breath turned to soft hiccups. I sat up, wiped the tears from my cheeks. I should stay in and mourn, I thought.

But then, with certainty, I thought, *No. I will go. I want to celebrate life—hers, and mine while I still have it. I want to live a full life, like she did.* I was about to go out to a noisy, impersonal party. But for me, now, the celebration was very personal.

I got up and walked into the kitchen, my boots *tap tap tapping* on the wooden floor. Selecting my favorite tiny glass from the cupboard, I returned to the now-completely dark living room. I opened the whiskey bottle, poured myself a shot, then closed the bottle. The stars in the sky mirrored the lights of the city along the inky black bay.

I took a breath. I raised the glass to the sky. "To you, Oma," I said. "Thank you. I will remember."

Adirondack Chairs
by Christina Kemp

Empty house. After someone leaves. Funny how your presence moved things.

Evening sunlight is dappling through the trees across the street. So tall, the evergreens. I hadn't really noticed the way their branches smile subtly upward toward the sky. Makes me think of a painting, of Bob Ross. *Happy trees.* That gentle sound of tapping brush, thick and wet, heavy bristle meeting canvas...

And those soft allowances. Spaces for breath.

Wind chimes from my neighbor's house across the street offer their serene tinkling as the breeze gently caresses itself through tall stretching trees on the surrounding acres. The swaying, long and together, offers sounds I have not yet heard, as the wind takes precedence over birdsongs normally filling the air.

Last night was thick gray, humid, and still, and I spoke with the farmer nearby about thunderstorms coming. The ions release something for us, a new charge.

Even animals know and become quieted.

I've moved to an island, and the people who pass my street are neighborly. Everyone knows everyone, it seems, at the end of this farm road. When you visited over the weekend, I watched as you stood gaily at the window, waving to those passing by.

The first morning after you arrived, I could hear the stairway creak as you descended from the harbor of my upstairs guestroom and small attic library where my books are stacked on every shelf and quotes are written in cursive shorthand on small bits of paper pinned to the walls. You came into the kitchen in pale pajamas and a floral robe, me in my sweats and a tee, barefoot, pulling those blueberry muffins you love from the oven. Sister-like friends, the two of us sat at my old patio table on the back porch, spreading warm butter and interweaving conversation with sips of tea throughout the morning, discussing lovers, recipes, and what life has held since we were last together.

And then we leaned back and looked over the small pieces of grass blowing in the wind. Revering ourselves in the unknown that is yet to come. And feeling the comfort of being together, all the same.

When I first moved here, I was overwhelmed by the work that needed to be done. Intimidated, for weeks I walked the periphery of my property, finger tapping and playing at my mouth, as I thought about a plan and considered my own anxieties. Outside, I stood and stared at the enormity of a blackberry bush in its fullness, all of its thorns and thrush in rapid expansion, overtaking the side of my house with its climbing, adhesive branches.

You came to help me get settled here—on this island where I have been wanting to root.

Before your arrival, I began removing the bush. I thought to only try a few stems with the shears, but it wasn't long until I was engrossed in the process: pulling, trimming, cutting, clearing further and further, enamored in wonderment with the tangible visibility of my work.

It quieted all of my hunger.

When you pull something out by its roots, the ground makes the most wonderful sound—the earthy woodiness releasing its grip, dirt reconfiguring itself, sifting, finding momentary flight as you jerk what you hold from the ground.

The roots of weeds go deep, and I found some too far beneath the ground to firmly grasp and adhere to with all my might. I clipped them deep in the dirt, allowing them to rest a while longer. I know sometimes we can't get to the bottom of what we want to dispel, and I suppose the earth was telling me to trust its hold a season or two longer. Perhaps, even more.

"We must respect people's defenses." A wise woman once said this. I was thinking of how many defenses I wanted to climb and overturn within myself, but the memory of her statement made me take pause.

I covered the remaining lodged roots with mulch and left them for next season.

When the bulk of the bush was cleared, its leaves and branches laid scattered over my lawn, wilting in the sun. I didn't mind the scratches, the dirt in my eyes and hair that washed away easily that evening. But the release that came from that work, the *relief*. Places unseen that needed to be aired out, newly felt; sifting through my fingers, falling discarded; and then left alone for a while.

Tending movements, done through the work of dirt.

"I wonder now, how I got along so far without this," I said, kale leaves on a fork, sitting at lunch with you, sipping a Pellegrino. I motioned my head to the leaves blowing gently in the wind outside the open doors of the restaurant.

We spoke about the workings of the inner life and how the earth resonates, meeting us in places beneath conscious thought, rich minerals absorbing through the skin and rejuvenating dusty corners of the soul, replenishing what has been seeping out through the years.

We finished our salads and walked arm in arm down the quiet two-lane street, peering through windows and sauntering through the small shops in town.

Later that afternoon, the breezes off of the shore swept in and moved through the country grasses around the house, tickling strands of hair into our eyes, as we sat on the fresh cut pasture, leaning back, our fingers barely touching, our minds out of the thoughts of clouds.

On the second day, we stubbed our toes at identical moments. I whispered *fuck* under my breath, and you echoed an *oh my god, ouch!* in the other room. We listened, and then laughed. Funny twinning moment. Two girls of blonde.

You fixed the misaligned slats in my wooden chairs—so we could lean into their embrace under that night's expansive net of stars—and helped reconfigure a firepit by the fence of an overgrown pasture with apple trees. The dry hot dust of summer floated up to meet our glistening faces and watering eyes, as we dug discarded blue and yellow tiles out of the ground and secured them next to large rocks to contain the fires to come, ants scurrying at our feet. Fatigued labor at the end of the day, lending to frustration, our bodies bent in uncomfortable positions amid earth that didn't want to move. We finished, leaving one rock sitting oddly out of place.

There is a small cluster of old trees across the property line just beyond the field, and I've paused in captivating moments to take them in—as they stand, steady and wise against the sky. We remarked on their sage presence as we threw large pieces of dry wood into the fire, over the small crackling branches, spreading smoke before it burst fully into flame. The smell of burning wood released into the air as the evening, open and gazing, fell deeper into shades of blue, the cool air settling around us. I adjusted on the Adirondack as the wood slats creaked, and a cricket spoke a gentle song amid the ascending night sky.

I know the trees are not old growth, but they seem to have survived long enough to have taken substantial root.

Winds changing over time will do this.

It doesn't take much to adhere to what's beneath; and in the process, to deepen alongside each other.

I'll always remember the way you carried me, many years ago, as we flew down open city roads, the day the news of my cancer came. Windows open, hair in the air. The allowances you gave me through the moments that followed—clumsy, fragmented, and lacking grace. You were gentle and supporting. Trying and uncertain, not always knowing what to say.

But still you stayed.

I remembered that while we walked our last afternoon together, in the coolness under the canopy of forest. The relief the varying shades of green brought from the high daylight sun. I stood planted on the dirt path. Images of that summer long ago danced before me as the waving leaves played timelessly, the way you stood and walked with me, and walk and stand with me still.

This is what we get when we stretch the years together and don't lose contact. When we remain together through the moments that bend our spirits, but where we find life rich and full of meaning, all the same.

We become familiar.

Bare feet step across the floor, and someone sighs some soft undertone of feeling from another room—

And that feeling of home comes back to greet us.

There is something sacred in the ordinary, in what we have earned together through all the years, gifts I hold with an open hand.

Even though we will always have to let go of what we love in order to keep it near, and there is no joy in saying goodbye.

Quiet heaviness fell between us in the short drive back toward the dock. Sadness in our parting, neither of us wanted you to leave. We sat for a moment, looking out the windows, before lifting ourselves to embrace and say goodbye. I told you I loved you and you said the same. You're on the ferry now, making your way back to the city. Friends and family to see.

I opened the front door to the quiet sadness that follows whenever a loved one leaves. Maybe it is only in the eternal that we find our way back to each other with the permanence craved by the spirit. The way we come so close, and then we are stretched further apart. And all the while, we try through an endurance of the years not to let go of those we believe we are meant for; however transient and short-lived the moments together may seem.

Those swaying trees are enclosing their fingering roots to-gether—holding on—far underground from what we see.

Down on the carpet is a small outline of your bag. I turn toward the attic, where my cat brushes past my leg as she runs up the stairs to the guestroom. I follow and see sunlight pour-ing through a room now made different by your presence. I sit on the edge of the bed, the cat rubbing herself against the an-tique frame; my hand rests on the soft grey quilt. I decide to leave the room untouched a few days longer, to ease the ab-sence of your parting.

As I make my way back down, the stairs creak in what are beginning to feel like familiar sounds from long worn crevices of this hundred-year-old house.

I stand in the silence for a moment, feeling the waning of your presence. My chest aches with that eternal remembering of what will never leave, but which is now out of reach for this moment. There is a presence of your absence, *all of your absences—*

You whom I love, but am apart from, for a time.

The Earth's spinning is never-ending, and moves us on. I feel you again before letting go, as I head toward the kitchen, fingers trailing the empty air, the cat scampering in front of me. Dark bananas are sitting where I left them to ripen on the counter, and I peel them back to bake them into bread. I know they will infuse me with a familiar, similar resonance of warmth and comfort that will last momentarily, and also even-tually pass.

I can walk down the quiet of my street in the early evening, then. And listen to the birds.

Never Heard
by Rebecca Mabanglo-Mayor

There's a story I never heard as a child, a story about a girl who fell from the sky to the Earth below before there was land.

She fell toward a vast sea and would have drowned if not for the kindness of ducks, the wisdom of Grandmother Turtle, and the tenacity of Old Toad. It's the falling that always captures my imagination, no matter which version I hear or read—Tagalog, Muscogee, Oneida. Maybe she dug the hole she fell through herself. Maybe someone dug it for her. Doesn't matter because she's falling—falling away from her home in the sky and everything she knows and loves. She's falling but too startled to comprehend that she's in trouble, that she may die, that she may never return home. She's looking up to the sky even as her body is falling to the Earth, nothing in her mind at all except the sensation of weightlessness and the sight of the hole she fell through getting smaller and smaller.

Eyes wide. Arms wheeling slowly. Hair across her gaped mouth. A scream. Or perhaps a cry forced back into her throat with the wind.

And I wonder: what is it like to not know your fate, to simply fall into a new life?

Then I think of another story I never heard, the one about my grandfather, Lolo Sylvestre. He left the family plantation in Santa Cruz, Zambales, Philippines, one day when he was sixteen. The day could have been rainy or clear. He could have left at an easy pace or on quick feet as if pursued. Maybe he walked across the raised path between green rice paddies surrounded by mango and papaya trees. Maybe he carried a pack of food or believed he could find work as he walked south toward Manila. Whatever the case, he never looked back.

One day more than a generation later, my father and I sat in the kitchen together, a gold Formica counter between us. He sipped Sanka from a white mug and I drank water from a glass that matched the counter. He told me what he'd pieced together about his own father, Sylvestre, and his grandmother.

"His father died," said my father. "My *Lola*, she was a Mayor, then she remarried and became a Mas. We have relatives who are Mas in Zambales." He nodded once and looked out the kitchen window as if to see the past. "My grandfather, your great-grandfather was Catholic, but Mas was not. *Iglesia de Cristo*." He nodded once again at the truth of his thoughts. "My father left and never went back. My brothers and I didn't know we had relatives in Zambales until I was sixteen myself. I went all the way north to visit the family I didn't know. When I first met my cousins, the children of my father's stepsister and brothers, they all prayed for me. They cried, they were so happy to see me. They thought my father had died.

They said my father didn't like that he couldn't be Catholic anymore."

I imagined that my great-grandmother's new family believed that they would all burn in Hell if they didn't convert to her husband's faith and worship God properly. Sylvestre's stepfather probably didn't believe that his wife's first children were Christians—the Catholic rituals were too close to paganism for his comfort.

We can't be sure why he left; he kept his reasons secret, never telling his family in Calapan, Mindoro, of his family in Santa Cruz, Zambales, two hundred-thirty miles away.

Perhaps he wasn't like the girl who fell from the sky unwillingly and by accident. It simply may have been time for him to seek his fortune. Maybe he was more like the woman who fell because she was curious about the world below, the woman whom Thomas King named Charm.

Charm lived in the sky and became pregnant. She craved the roots of a particular tree and when she dug the hole, she dug deep enough to poke a hole through the sky. She bent down to see what was on the other side and, despite the warnings of creatures above, looked too deeply and fell to the Earth below. She never returned to the sky, but lived on an island on a turtle's back, her curiosity the cause of her great change.

Whatever the reason for his leaving, he never returned to the plantation in Santa Cruz, Zambales, even though he lived to his mid-sixties, raised eight boys, and watched his grandchildren grow up in houses built around his own. His family in Zambales imagined the worst until word returned that the son of the son-who-had-left was returning home, returning to them. My father left his hometown of Calapan, Oriental Mindoro, at the age of sixteen. A cousin in Manila wrote a letter asking if he would visit her, and when he arrived, asked why his father never went back to his family to the north.

"My father, my *tatay*, never told us about the family he left behind," he said, his shoulders lifting as he turned to pour himself another cup of coffee. "He wrote letters to them. My cousin said so. But he never said anything to us."

"Why?"

Dark coffee still filled his mug and he took a tentative sip, then shook his head as he set the mug back on the counter. I left my water alone and watched his thoughts play over his dark eyes.

Perhaps my father's mind was like the wheeling arms of the girl, thoughts tumbling, speculating about the people he did not know. He never asked his father why he had left home, but perhaps my father understood the heart of a sixteen-year-old as he himself made the journey back to the plantation. My father left his home too, and his journey took him even farther from Calapan. He tried selling shoes door-to-door and failing that, joined the US Navy. He travelled the world from North Pole to South Pole and points between until finally he met a Filipina in Seattle, married her, and raised my brother and me.

And I wonder: what is it like to make the choice to leave the only home you know and make a life in a foreign place?

When I think about the girl who fell from the sky, her story is more like my mother's story. Her father was in the US Army after serving as a Philippine Scout and surviving the Bataan Death March. His dream was the American Dream and after the Korean War, he moved his wife and six daughters to Seattle. His eldest, my mother, was twenty and halfway through college when he made this decision. She had a college degree in pharmacy to complete, a boyfriend, and a slew of girlfriends who would sneak out of the dormitory with her to see Clark Gable kiss Vivien Leigh at the movies. She had every reason to stay in Dagupan City, but she boarded the *USS Barrett* as her father had arranged. Instead of a flotilla of helpful ducks to guide her toward the Earth, mother had a ship made of steel bound for San Francisco. A train took her north to Seattle. She looked forward to Washington apples and was excited to see the December snows, but then the cold Seattle rains of January chilled her blood and she longed for home.

She reeled at the changes she encountered in the New World—no helpful maids to do her washing. Strange men with bulky bodies called 'football players.' The possibility of rape in the face of every male stranger she encountered on the bus, at school, in Chinatown. The uncertainty that she was a strong, intelligent woman in the face of "equal opportunity quotas." Although my father often talked about going back to the Philippines permanently and my mother balked at the idea at each turn, I think she often looked back to her life in Dagupan like the ever-receding hole in the sky, never able to really go back to the girl she once was.

And when I ask myself why I write, and the story of the falling girl comes to mind, I realize that I write to save these family stories I heard from my mom while I dried dishes in the kitchen or over breakfast with my dad as he poured sugar-free creamer into his Sanka. My father reads Pinoy newspapers and my mother reads books by Carl Sagan and Richard Feynman, but neither of them writes. I write their stories ever conscious that they are not my stories and there is always the risk of getting them wrong. Then again, better wrong than forgotten. Someone must trace the movements of the sky on cloudy days before the time when land was formed.

There's a story I never heard as a child about a girl who fell from the sky to the Earth below before there was land to break up the vast sea. A story about kind ducks, a wise turtle, and a tenacious toad. A story about the girl who became the first woman who lived on a round island created on a turtle's back out of dirt pulled from the bottom of the sea. In some retellings, there are twins born on the island who are the Left Hand of Chaos and the Right Hand of Creation.

And I think about how I didn't have this story when I was growing up—instead my mother read me stories about Mother Goose, a mouse who learned how to be a good big brother, and a little girl in a blue dress who generously shared her fifth birthday with her neighbors. I learned how to build sentences as we crossed the Pacific Ocean one December to celebrate my father's graduation from college with a trip to the Philippines. I read about Dick and Jane and their dog, Spot, and heard the flow of sentences like musicians hear phrases of song. I felt the structure of the narrative like architects imagine skyscrapers as yet unbuilt. I saw words as pictures like painters see landscapes. I fell in love with stories headlong like the girl falling through a hole in the clouds.

One Christmas two years after that trip abroad, I bought my first book, *The Lion, the Witch, and the Wardrobe,* with my Christmas gift money. My mother would have rather I saved the funds for college ten years in the future, but I was entranced with Lewis's story that my third-grade teacher read to us a chapter at a time. I had to have my own copy. I had to have my own passage to Narnia.

No, more than that—I had to possess Narnia itself, to talk with fauns and child-kings, beavers and centaurs, to fight great battles with only a sword at my side (no bow and arrow for me), and survive to tell the tales. As I stood at the bookstore counter with trembling hands and my small pink wallet, I realized the thin book with the pale blue spine was only the first of seven in the series, that there were more adventures to come, and then in the vastness of a bookstore, I could possess other worlds with the simple flip of a coin.

Yes, I loved libraries and the freedom to pick stories about children living in boxcars or in attics to hide from the Nazis with nothing more than a library card, but borrowing was altogether different from owning a book. I'd have to give those stories back to give someone else a chance to read them. I'd have to trust my memory of exactly how the coats in the wardrobe felt as Lucy pushed past them, what the sound of the stone altar breaking in two beneath the dead body of Aslan was exactly as Lewis described it. I wanted to possess the books and worlds completely like the greedy, imaginative explorer I was.

Soon I had the complete Narnia set and then began reading and collecting Tolkien. Then Anne McCaffrey and Ursula K. Le Guin, Roger Zelanzy, and Mary Stewart. Even the novelizations of the Star Wars series. I shelved my books on my gold-gilt French Provincial desk and wrote fan-fiction on green steno pads my dad brought from the office. Later I borrowed his Corona typewriter and applied my piano keyboard skills to move the keys that struck the paper with a satisfying *clack*. Each book I bought was a doorway to the worlds I loved better than the world I lived in as a Filipino girl growing up in an all-white neighborhood and going to parochial school where being in the minority meant being one of a handful of children who's skin lacked the creamy pinkness of the characters I read in my treasured books.

There were no stories to prepare me for being a girl of color growing up to be a woman of color so it was easier for me to imagine myself to be like the people I saw every day, not just the students in my math and science classes, but the people on TV and movies. I could be strong and smart like the Bionic Woman or Wilma Deering. I could captain a starship, wield a lightsaber, meet aliens with rainbow suspenders. I could dance with Gene Kelley, sing with Julie Andrews, and cry over my dead (imagined) boyfriend with Maria in the empty schoolyard. Their stories over-wrote my experiences because I had no language to describe being that A+, piano-playing, suburban Filipino-American who remained invisible on the fringe. I fell so far from my being that I believed I could become Carl Sagan himself if I studied astronomy and physics in college. I didn't realize that it was the Ship of the Imagination I wanted to fly, to tell stories to a greater audience that I wanted from his career, his story.

And when I ask myself why I write and I think about how the girl who fell from the sky became part of a new community that physically resembled her very little, I realize I'm trying to describe what it's like to be a human riding the back of a turtle, living in the company of Old Toad, Clever Rat, and Bright-Eyed Kingfisher. I'd like the ability to dive deep, to be bold, to have precise will, but I'm just a girl who fell in love with stories but forgot my own. So I write to remember myself, to tell me the one story no one else can tell.

There's a story I never heard as a child but one I've told my children and the children in my audiences for the past decade. It's the story of the girl who fell from a hole in the sky, and sometimes she's looking for healing and sometimes she's curious about the world below and sometimes we don't know why she fell, only that she's falling. And in the story, there are ducks or some such helpful flock of birds to ease her passage into the new world, chattering, fluffy Midwives of Change who find the wisdom to solve the problem of this human landing on the earth. And even though it's usually Grandmother Turtle who gathers the People together to help the girl, sometimes it's Old Toad who brings back mud in his mouth and sometimes it's Reluctant Otter who brings up magic soil between her claws, but in all the Tellings, the People spread the mud on Grandmother's back and make a place for the girl to live and raise her family.

And I think that's really why I write and perform—I'm making an island for the people who've fallen, who find themselves falling for whatever reason—oppression, addiction, disappointment, disability—so they'll know they're not alone, that they can survive the trauma of their past and make sense of themselves. And if they're not alone, then neither am I, and we can build doorways to fantastic worlds and look at each other to say, "Wow, that was cool. Let's do it again!" Because you see, that turtle isn't floating in space. She's standing on another turtle who's standing on another turtle and you could say that it's turtles all the way down.

But that's a different story.

Resilience
by Judith Mayotte

Most of the women I met in refugee camps around the world
had lived ten, twelve, even fifteen years in the camps or in
sordid urban situations. Some were relegated to places where
even a cockroach would find it difficult to survive. Yet, for
the most part, survive they did. Many even flourished and
found new ways to move forward with their lives. Their raw
stories of life and death—so different from any experiences
I'd ever had—motivated me to continue my work as an advocate on their behalf.

I often think of a group of midwives I visited in the early
1990s in southern Sudan while on a fact-finding mission for
the Women's Refugee Commission with my colleague, Kathleen Jacobs. Upon our return to the United States, we would
be tasked to speak publicly about the dire situation in southern
Sudan. We would write op-ed pieces, testify before the House
and/or Senate Foreign Relations Committee, and document in
a report our findings and recommendations that we could
disseminate to government and United Nations High Com-

missioner for Refugees (UNHCR) officials, and humanitarian organizations.

By the time I first set foot on Sudanese soil, Sudan had been in the throes of civil conflict for years. In fact, civil strife began in 1956, the year Sudan became independent from Britain. There was an eleven-year hiatus from conflict between 1972 and 1983, but then war again broke out with a vengeance. The government of Sudan fought fiercely against the southern Sudanese, Sudan People's Liberation Army (SPLA). Government forces found that withholding access to food and medical assistance became just as effective in achieving their ends against the civilian population as guns and mortars.

Humanitarian aid organizations were frequently forced to leave the south and even their attempts to deliver airdrops of life-saving grain were thwarted. In the years following 1983, southern Sudan even experienced a civil war within a civil war—Riek Machar, a leader from the Nuer tribe, split from the SPLA leadership of John Garang, a Dinka tribesman. For a time, Machar and his troops defected to the government side, making access to life-saving aid even more difficult.

It was during the period of Machar's defection that Kathleen and I departed Nairobi's small Wilson Airport in a single engine, four-seater airplane. Few pilots were willing to carry humanitarian workers into southern Sudan, Ethiopia, Eritrea, or Somalia. Planes out of Wilson were generally hired for private safari parties traveling to see the African wildlife in their natural habitat. This particular morning, Kathleen and I were assigned a pilot originally from what had been southern Rhodesia, now Zimbabwe. He was quite familiar with the many nearby safari sites but had never before flown into the southern Sudan war zone. At this time, the government of Sudan was not allowing humanitarian assistance of either food or medical aid to reach the most vulnerable southern Sudanese people, in spite of the fact that every national sovereign has the responsibility to protect its citizens. By withholding life supporting aid, thousands of citizens living within the area held by the SPLA were dying of malnutrition or preventable diseases.

The moratorium on humanitarian aid meant our pilot had to make a clandestine approach, flying low across the border out of the range of government planes that could strafe our plane. He made his official flight plan to look like we would end on the Kenyan side of the border in the humanitarian base camp compound at Lokichoggio, but in reality we were headed for Nimule, a small town just across the border in a SPLA area of southern Sudan.

As we approached the area the pilot believed to be near Nimule, he turned to Kathleen and me and asked if either of us spotted a landing strip below. I pointed to a landing strip out my window, hoping we were in the right place. If our plane were shot down or if we were in government territory, the consequences could be life-threatening. As we flew lower and lower and approached the landing strip, we finally saw friendly waves by personnel from the International Rescue Committee (IRC).

Immensely relieved, and following a warm welcome, we clambered into the pickup truck for the short ride to the IRC compound. Once Kathleen and I had placed our belongings in our grass tukul where we would be sleeping, we immediately headed to meet with a group of midwives. There were about a dozen women gathered to meet with us. We sat on the dusty ground together. Kathleen and I listened to their stories of flight from place to place and their losses of husbands and children—either by death or by separation—amid the conflict. We listened to their hopes for a better future if—when—the fighting would cease and they could live peacefully in their villages once again. I saw strong women who individually and as a group were determined to move forward and not lose hope for a brighter day.

As my job as an advocate was to make the plight of these women known, I asked the group, "What message would you like for me to take back to people in the United States?"

One of the midwives stood and replied poignantly, "Tell them we are tired of running—running from bombardments, massacres, and starvation. Tell them we gather our children and try to find a place to hide in the bush. We look for water and try to stay awhile. But guns break the silence and we have to run again. We are tired of running."

These women, who were displaced within their own country, were still under the authority of the Sudanese government, which, with relentless malevolence, pursued them. They did not have the same protections as a refugee who crossed an international border and found asylum in a foreign country. Despite their dangerous situation, the strength, kindness, and determination of these midwives shone through, and I felt keenly my responsibility as an advocate for their humanity.

As our conversation with them closed, Kathleen and I noticed a chicken flopping around on the ground. As one of the women bent over to pick up the chicken, we saw that the chicken's legs were tethered. Holding the clucking chicken tightly, the woman approached us and handed the chicken to Kathleen. These midwives, who did not even have clean razor blades with which to cut the umbilical cord in the birthing process, much less enough food to properly nourish their children and themselves, gave Kathleen and me a precious chicken for our dinner. We wanted to refuse but knew that would be to insult the gift.

As we ate that night, both the plight and courage of the midwives dominated our dinner conversation.

Not long after sharing an afternoon with the midwives in southern Sudan, I flew on my own to Pakistan to spend time with another group of midwives in a refugee camp, outside of the city of Quetta, in a large border area in southwest Pakistan abutting Afghanistan. The women taught me vitally important lessons about the indispensable, time-honored human need for community and, yes, even laughter, pride, and song.

It was in Quetta that I first met up with Elisabeth Neuenschwander, a Swiss national humanitarian worker. I doubt that I will ever meet a stronger, more dedicated advocate for women and girls than Elisabeth. Even today in her nineties, Elisabeth's clarion call continues to ring out: "What about the women and girls?"

In the early morning, once Elisabeth and I were seated in the car and ready for the long drive to the refugee camp, our driver proceeded from Elisabeth's home to the lodgings of a woman named Nuria. Nuria slipped out of the house fully covered by her blue burka, a laced opening across her eyes allowing her to see where she was going. She wore her burka so as to be kept from sight by any male, as prescribed by the Afghan elders. Once Nuria joined us in the car, she pulled back the total covering so that her veiled head encompassed her thin face—aquiline nose and large, deep brown eyes. I could only see the dark brown hair just above her temples; the veil covered the rest of her long locks. Outgoing and talkative in precise British English, we never wanted for conversation on the remaining hour's ride beyond Quetta to the rural refugee camps.

Elisabeth and Nuria's histories were interesting and intertwined. Elisabeth was born in a Swiss village from which few ever strayed in a lifetime. But Elisabeth had bigger dreams than to stay in Switzerland. Once she completed her secondary education, Elisabeth set out to travel the globe. When she'd landed in the high, remote area of Hunza in northeastern Pakistan, the people and their needs captured her heart, especially the need for the education of young girls. There she developed schools for these girls.

Elisabeth was still in Hunza when she learned of the Soviet invasion of Afghanistan and the several million Afghans who fled the war to find refuge in the border areas of Pakistan, near either Peshawar or Quetta. Elisabeth said goodbye to her friends in Hunza and made her way south and west to Quetta and saw how Afghan men controlled the movement of the women. In exile, in the name of protection of the women, the men's hold became stronger than it would have been under normal circumstances. They built their compounds out of the brown earth of Pakistan and closed their families off inside the walls. The compounds typically consisted of the several wives of one man—who was generally off fighting in Afghanistan—the elderly men in the family, and myriad children belonging to the several wives.

Elisabeth saw two great needs in this community. One was for the women to be able to generate income, since their husbands were off fighting in the war. The second was the need for the children to be educated. Madrassas, Islamic religious schools, were set up for the boys, but the girls were denied even primary education. Undeterred, Elisabeth knew what she could do to deal with the men.

Elisabeth contacted the office of the United Nations High Commissioner for Refugees (UNHCR), and was able to obtain manual sewing machines that sat on the ground. With sewing machines, the women could make school uniforms for local Pakistani school children and warm quilts for refugees. To obtain a sewing machine, the male head of the compound or the leader of a group of Afghans living in a particular refugee camp had to give women under his authority his permission. Some men refused such permission—that is, until they saw other men allowing their women the machines. Once these recalcitrant men observed other men giving women permission to generate income, they, too, sought out Elisabeth to obtain the now-coveted sewing machines. Even though Afghan elders frowned upon women working, most families could survive only if the women worked.

Nuria became engaged with Elisabeth's work after her family had fled to seek refuge in Pakistan, settling in Quetta. She had been but a young girl when, in the middle of the night, Soviet backed militia members burst into their home in Lashkar Gah, the capital of Afghanistan's Helmand province, shackled her father, and took him away. Family members sought his prison location in vain. They did not even know if he was alive. Theirs had been a comfortable home in Afghanistan's geographically largest province located in the south of the country. But in spite of their comfort, their family was in danger. Nuria's father had worked for an American company and was suspect by the Soviet invaders.

Elisabeth, Nuria, and I went to one of the refugee camps in the rural area surrounding Quetta to meet with a group of midwives. The road to the camps was long, dusty, and rutted. In some places it was wide enough for one and a half cars, but certainly not for two. As our driver accelerated to a dangerous speed, I spied a bus not far ahead, coming toward us. Only once we were at a close range with the bus did our driver rapidly slow down and pull off to the side. He turned his head to us in the backseat and pointedly spoke two words, "Chicken play."

As he pulled back onto the road, he turned again to the three of us saying, "In Pakistan there are no rules of the road."

Elisabeth, Nuria, and I looked at each other and sighed in relief. Up ahead a cross-country bus sat motionless in the middle of the road. Our relief turned again to anxiety as we wondered if this was a bandit-backed roadblock—not uncommon in this area. Would we be robbed? Worse? Fortunately, the driver started the bus, pulled to the far side of the road, and let us pass.

When the car stopped, I observed the expansive refugee camp filled with mud compounds, packed closely together. An Afghan woman trained as a community health worker then led us by foot to a compound deep within the grounds. Outside, seated beside a dugout oven, a woman placed naan dough along the roasting, interior side of the oven. I found hot, fresh naan to be a treat through my various stays among the Afghans. Once we entered the mud house of one of the wives, we were greeted by a group of ten women, happily engaged in conversation.

The home was spotlessly clean. Colorful floor cushions abutted one wall, backed by other large colorful pillows, the Afghan version of our sofas. Off to one side I spied a few cooking pots, plates, cups, and other kitchenware nestled together. A well-worn trunk appeared to serve as a table as well as a storage chest. Two smaller trunks rested below a poster of a snow-clad mountain scene.

Among the chattering women were two midwives, there to hold a midwifery class to teach clean, healthy procedures for the birthing process. All too frequently, women died in childbirth. Traditionally, when a woman came to term and her water broke, she squatted over a hole carved in the middle of a room in her home. Once the baby emerged from the woman's womb, the person attending the birth would place a shoe over the umbilical cord to hold it down as she cut the cord with a razor. These actions, although traditional, were leading to infections and diseases in the context of the refugee camp.

As the two midwives began the class, three metal washbasins were placed in the center of the room. Hot water boiled over a portable burner. The midwives placed soap and clean rags beside one of the basins. A woman named Bakhtawar played the role of the midwife that day. As she came to the center of the room, she pulled back and secured the veil covering her head, rolled up the colorful sleeves of her traditional dress and pulled up her equally colorful embroidered, long, flowing skirt. She tied the rose-patterned, baggy pants tight at her ankles. Her large bare feet matched the dust of the floor.

Next, she carefully poured heated water into a basin and thoroughly scrubbed her hands and arms more than once. As she stood, she held her arms up and away from her body to maintain their sterility.

She then knelt carefully by Mastana, the woman who role-played a pregnant woman. Mastana lay prone on a clean plastic sheet. Once Bakhtawar determined it was time for the delivery of the baby, she crossed to the midwife's case and retrieved a skeleton pelvis and a doll baby with an umbilical cord tied around its neck. Bakhtawar returned to Mastana and, with sure-ty, "delivered" the baby through the skeleton cervical opening, unwrapped the umbilical cord from the baby's neck, and hand-ed the baby to the mother. When the newborn suddenly stopped breathing, Bakhtawar successfully breathed life back into the imaginary child. At this point, congratulations, smiles, and chatter rose from the other observing students.

One of the midwife instructors also taught the women the need for healthy birth-spacing. In order to quickly replace those lost in the war, women were impregnated at a rate too dangerous for their health. In this moment I could see how the political became the personal: women paid the price for the heavy casualties from a war not of their making.

With the class complete, the women socialized over hot tea heavy with sugar. Shyly, Bakhtawar approached me and asked if she could show me something. I followed her to her foot-locker from which she took her wedding dress. In flight, it was one treasure, so carefully preserved, she kept and brought with her into her long exile. The beauty of a more peaceful time shone through her elaborately decorated wedding dress. I felt keenly aware of the loss these women experienced, yet I sensed their hope for a better future.

As I spoke with her about her life, I wondered how I would fare if I were in her place, and in the place of refugee women around the world. How might I react to suddenly being up-rooted from a stable life raising children, caring for a husband, interacting with neighbors and friends? Would I be as resilient as they were if, daily, I had to run from shelling or cover my children with my body when bombs fell from the sky onto my neighborhood? What if soldiers came in the night, broke down the door to my home and took my husband away, and I didn't know where he was or what my next steps should be? Would I break, or would I have the strength to move forward? In such a circumstance, and being neither literate nor skilled enough to make a living for my family, how would I cope? How would I provide for the children? Would I survive living in a refugee camp for years? How would I receive the news my husband had been killed in battle?

These questions and so many more clamored for answers. Perhaps hardest was knowing that, unlike the women I encountered in war zones and refugee camps, I could always cross back over the River Styx. I could cross out of the underworld and back into the safety of a homeland not at war, a country from which I did not have to flee in order to save my life and the life of my family. These women, so resilient, embodied the reality that the prosperity of a community rests with the health of the women, and their fullest vitality is contingent on peace.

Violence
by G. Annie Ormsby

My dad's two expat friends, Jerry and Rene, who lived in Mexico full time, gave strict instructions for the two-day drive from Nogales, Arizona, to Tepic, Nyarit, Mexico, where they would be waiting to meet us and take us to the doctor they'd arranged to see Dad. "Do not leave the toll highway, do not drive past dark, drive directly, with only one or two stops a day solely at the gas stations connected to the highway, and drive fast to make it to the safe house arranged for you midway from the border." This was no joke, they'd said. The US government was currently moving Sinoloa and Sonora, the two northern states that we would be traveling through, from a Stage 3 to a Stage 4 travel advisory, putting them on par with Afghanistan and Somalia in terms of the danger factor for foreigners.

So far, it seemed that somebody was watching out for us. Before we even got to Mexico, while arriving in Nogales, Arizona, the 2005 Honda Accord we were driving suddenly began chugging and sputtering. An elderly Hispanic man, who overheard me telling my story to the clerk at the Auto Zone

store, arranged an immediate appointment at his buddy's re-
pair shop. With only one day lost, we crossed the US border
in our smooth-running car. Fortune changed, though, when we
were only twelve miles into Mexico. We were denied any
forward access at a second border check.

The car we were in was borrowed from my father's girlfriend, Patty. Our names were not on its title. So early in our
journey and it looked like we could go no farther, until a
shady character scoping the parking lot sold us what he
claimed was a legitimate "access sticker" for an outrageous
number of US dollars. This documentation was meant to give
us a go-ahead at any checkpoint we would encounter between
here and our final destination. I was dubious about its legiti-
macy, but I decided to believe it would be sufficient. We were
in a hurry.

Five days earlier, Dad's jeep had overheated the first day of
our journey, before we were even able to get out of our home
state of Washington. We'd circled back home to figure out
what to do, and his girlfriend's car was the only viable option.
Maybe it was a sign we shouldn't take this trip, but Dad insisted on starting again, although he refused to buy the car from his
girlfriend so we could prove ownership, granting us the right to
drive it if we were stopped along the way.

"Please, Annie. Let's go," he'd said, so I agreed. He was
my only dad, and I was his only child. And now, together, we
were international felons having entered Mexico in a car that
looked stolen with an illegal sticker from an illegal coyote.
How stupid could I be?

It was about four hours after passing through the border
check that I stopped glancing in the mirrors every five seconds to see if anyone was coming for us. Just when I began to

breathe easier, I noticed the line of brake lights appear and a makeshift roadblock slowly emerge into view in front of us. When we'd inched to the front of the line, a dark-uniformed officer shined a light onto our pass on the windshield, regarded each of us slowly, then directed us to pull over to the left. Everyone else was going to the right.

I felt panic rising as my mind went wild with terrible scenarios, and I considered our options. My dad would never survive an arrest and detention, and my daughters needed their mother, so I stopped where they told me to—between two awaiting guards in wrinkly white button down shirts—and decided my best defense would be playing dumb. They opened our doors and motioned for us to get out, speaking rapidly in Spanish, a language I barely understood. One of them grabbed my dad's phone from his lap.

I looked at my waifish Pop, hunched over with the black cotton baseball cap he always wore to hide his thinning hair pulled down low over his eyes.

"Wait, wait," I yelled. *"Mi papá está muy enfermo,"* not knowing for sure if I was communicating what I wanted to with my first-year Spanish. "Cancer, cancer."

They both stopped pulling at us and yelled back to another officer whom I could see through my rearview mirror. His posture was strong and his countenance direct and clear. A relief washed over me. If it came down to us being arrested, I could give myself up to this man if I had to. But not with these other two. With their harsh sounds and brutish clawing-like movements, that would be accepting a defeat I could not abide. I got out of the car and stood to better observe the man whom I decided was worthy of deciding our fate. He met my gaze and no one moved for a full beat. He yelled something to the officer on my side who then began pushing me back into the car. I stood another moment before I sat back down in the driver's seat. Praying silently to whatever gods would listen, I reached out to my father who was holding onto the dashboard with both hands, his jaw clenching in rhythm with his labored breaths. He was eyeing his phone that the officer guarding his side of the car held in his hand.

The officer in the dark uniform, whom I later discovered was named Sebastian, made his way to my door. Motionless, he looked at me and took a couple of deep breaths, then he spoke into the walkie-talkie device affixed to his shoulder and leaned into the car.

"Tell him I need my phone," my dad grumbled in my ear.

With my tightened throat, I focused on Sebastian.

"What is the problem? *Mi papá-cancer. Muy enfermo.*"

He shone his flashlight on my sticker again and shook his head. "No good. Fake," he said.

"What?" I countered, putting a look of utter incredulity on my face. In a way, it was an authentic response. We had paid good money for that sticker. Fuck you, coyote man, I fumed inside. Fuck you. "I don't understand. *No comprendo,*" I said shaking my head and patting my father's back as he coughed and wheezed.

"*Mi papá,*" I said in a more pleading voice. "Doctor in Nyarit. Tepic. Cancer."

He looked out again toward the horizon and spoke into his walkie-talkie. "You. Wait here. Then, drive. Follow me." He spoke in labored English. I nodded.

"*Sí. ¿El teléfono?*" I gestured toward the other officer who was still standing outside my dad's open door holding his phone hostage. Sebastian nodded in his direction, and the man gave the phone back. There was nothing I could do but what I was told, so we followed Sebastian's cruiser for about five miles to a flat plot of dry land surrounded by a chain link fence topped with razor wire. The entrance had road spikes to prevent exiting. The feeling of absolute dread ran through me as I took in this desolate place.

Except for a 1980s Toyota hatchback parked in the back corner of the dusty gravel expanse that worked as a parking lot, ours were the only vehicles. In the middle of the lot stood an enormous light post with wheels at the base and four large halogen lights at the top. I felt the bump as we ran over the cord that went from it to a small shed nestled between two trailers facing each other. It was like some outdoor IKEA showroom; quick and easy assembly and disassembly.

I parked next to Sebastian and left our car running as there was no shade and the air conditioning felt life preserving. Dad's coughing fit while we were following Sebastian had left him struggling for air and banging on his chest as if to dislodge the tumor that grew there. Now he was exhausted and sucking on his inhaler.

On the way to this empty parking lot, he had tried to call Jerry and Rene, but no one answered, and, because of his coughing, I yelled into the phone an urgent voice mail explaining our circumstance. We could only hope that they would receive it soon and know what to do. Now Dad's phone sat on the console. We did not think to check its battery or to plug it in. Sebastian made his way over and asked me with simple words and signs to turn off the car and give him the keys. Reluctantly, I complied.

"Come, come. Papers? passports?" he said, beckoning me to follow.

"*Sí, sí. Mi papá aquí por favor?*" Could my father stay in the car, I wanted to know. He nodded okay, and I followed him up the ramp leading to a double-wide trailer on the far left end of the lot. I noted that a similar structure on the right had barred windows and a door that was locked with a chain. Ascending toward the entrance, I took in a quick overview of the grounds from my new perspective. They were desolate save one singular movement. There, among the small thorny bushes and cacti, was a man winding like a snake. He had no tools or any other outward clues as to what his role might be. In fact, he looked out of place with dirty clothes and unkempt hair. He cocked his head and walked sideways toward us as if to eavesdrop. I tensed and hoped Dad had locked the Honda's doors.

Sebastian guided me inside. The makeshift office's décor consisted of items in various hues of dirt. Prudent, I thought, as a cloud of dust followed us in. Though it was looking grim, I decided to stick to my story of ignorance.

Sebastian waited to be acknowledged by a small group of people—two women and a man—inside the building, and then, in a steady tone spoke to them, occasionally gesturing in my direction. I stood there, trying to look innocent. A man behind a desk asked Sebastian some questions as did a woman with long bright nails. I hoped our destiny did not now lie with her. She raised a perfectly coiffed eyebrow, shook her head in disgust and went about her work. The man at the desk regarded me with bemusement and got up to depart from the building, laughing as he left. That left a tiny woman with warm eyes, who gestured for me to come forward. As she began to peruse my papers, Sebastian considered his watch, said goodbye, and proceeded to the door.

"Wait, wait." I said. "*Mi papá.* Keys."

"*Está bien. Aquí.*" He handed me his card, exchanged pleasantries with the two women, and departed with my keys in his pocket. What the hell?

I smiled at the woman before me. She smiled back then glanced at the clock. Five pm. This was not good; darkness was looming. I repeated my simple tale. My father, who had stage IV lung cancer and could not fly, and I were traveling to Tepic to meet his friends and a doctor. We were driving his girlfriend's car. We thought the sticker was okay. Really. I then attempted, to no avail, to give her Dad's girlfriend's letter giving us permission to drive the car and her phone number so they could verify my story. I could not quite tell if she understood even some of what I said.

"Sorry," she said, and shrugged slowly to indicate there was nothing she could do. She handed back my papers and grabbed her phone and purse to get ready to leave.

"*No comprendo.*" I piled the papers together. I sat for a moment dumbfounded while she made for the back door. There, she stopped and pointed toward the front entrance, gesturing for me to leave as well. Not knowing what else to do, I left. This was all so befuddling.

Coming down the ramp, I saw my dad. He was on the phone waving his arms and shaking his head. I opened the driver's door. The hot air pulled me in and smothered me in its soup. I searched the grounds for the snake man and found him about ten yards off fingering a small shrub and considering us sideways.

"Here," my dad croaked, shoving the phone at me. Rene was on the line, and he sounded as worried as I was. I explained what had happened, and he told me to take the phone back into the trailer where he would see what headway he could make with the only person who, at this point was still there: the woman with the colorful nails. I told him that she did not seem friendly, but that Sebastian did, and he had our car keys. I read the information off of Sebastian's card. Rene said he would try to call a judge he knew and see if law enforcement could reach out to Sebastian, then he would call us back.

My dad's already frail frame was sunken and limp; his head rested on the door window. I gazed at his blazing white sneakers and ironed shirt and jeans. He worked so hard to keep up his appearance. My heart filled.

"Do you want us to give ourselves up and tell them we bought the illegal sticker and see what happens?" I asked. We both knew detainment would probably kill him, and that he would never survive a drive back. He pursed his lips and shook his head. I handed him his phone back and his eyes grew wide.

"The battery's at six percent," he stammered.

"Shit." Without a phone, no one would know what became of us. I shuddered thinking about the statistic I had recently read: only three percent of homicides were solved in Mexico.

"Quick, bring up all of the numbers," I said, scrambling to locate a pen and paper in Dad's black bag. I pulled out a set of keys. Dad's full set from home. We both froze.

"What the hell?" I said as I looked for one that fit the Accord. His girlfriend had given us her key when we left. Maybe Dad had his own copy?

"Okay, okay," I said, glancing up at the camera affixed to the corner of the trailer and pointing in our direction. "If we turn on the car, they might see or hear us and take our keys away. Let's just turn on the electrical to charge the phone and get some air. Fuck, fuck, fuck." It was the first time I had expressed my sense of futility in front of my father, and I regretted it immediately.

He reacted with physical distress, struggling to breathe, heaving his shoulders, while squeaking out words about the heat, the phone, and the lateness of the hour. Sweat dripped from his forehead through his closely trimmed greying beard and down his neck.

"Okay, okay. It's okay, Dad. It's all going to be all right." Snake man slithered toward our car. I checked the doors, turned the key, plugged in the phone and welcomed the air conditioning. It was not cold, but it was at least a fan. Snake man turned to face us several feet from my window. Fuck. I closed my eyes to try and will Rene to call. Time crept along. After what felt like fifteen minutes, I heard my dad mumble something.

"What did you say?"

"I'm going to call Patty." And he dialed her number.

I glared at him ready to scream at him about his priorities when a loud bang behind me on my window stopped me short. Someone was banging on our car, yelling something at me.

"Shit, Dad. Get off the phone." She was yanking on my door handle. When I unlocked it, she pulled it open with a massive force.

"*Vamos.*" She was an impatient mother and we her naughty kids. I stole a look at my dad, who was sitting back, eyes like griddle cakes.

"*Está muy enfermo,*" I reiterated, pointing at my father. She threw back her head and stomped to his side.

"*Vamos,*" she yelled. My dad inched his way into the burning sun. I got out and ran to help him onto the gravel. He clutched his phone and rocked meekly back and forth. The woman rolled her eyes, shook her head, and harrumphed with a dramatic flourish. She grabbed my dad's black bag and threw it out of the car onto the ground next to him.

"¡*Todos*!" she yelled again, indicating everything in the car and looking at me. I grabbed all of the items in the vehicle and placed them next to Dad. She tramped over to the trunk. "¡*Todos*!"

I took out the suitcases, bags of reading materials, Dad's cache of medications, the boxes of medical records, and his extra bedding. All of it lay there melting in the sun, like Dali's *Persistence of Memory*. I found a plastic bottle of water for Dad while she rifled through the bags, leaving the contents spread about the dusty gravel and concrete. I had no energy left but to pick up a pitched shirt and hold it up to shield my father from the sun. For what must have been almost an hour we watched as she explored every item and probed each and every seam, carpet, and mat inside the car.

"Where are the drugs?" she screamed in heavy accented English.

She thought we had drugs? That's what all of this was about? "There are no drugs. We just want to see the doctor in Tepic. My father has cancer."

"Give it up. Where are the drugs? Give them up. It's not worth it!" Her arms punctuated every word and her eyes grew rounder than I thought possible. What did she mean it's not worth it? What was she trying to tell us? And, when had she become such a good English speaker? She'd feigned ignorance when I'd tried to explain our situation before. But now I thought to try and reason with her again.

"Please. We are telling the truth. There are no drugs. My father is sick. This is his girlfriend's car. Please call her." I tried to hand her Dad's phone. We were poor simple pilgrims trying to make our way to the Holy Land. Damn it. Please, let us pass.

When she found nothing, she let out a visceral yell and stomped back into the trailer leaving us adrift among our flotsam and jetsam. I helped my dad back into the car and as quickly as I could, reloaded everything. I had seen snake man, whom I'd been keeping an eye on, disappear during the woman's performance, and now his whereabouts were a mystery. Back inside the car, doors locked, I decided to fully start the car. We were dying of heat, damn it.

Nothing. The battery was dead. And I panicked for real now.

"What the hell? Dad? Try Rene!" Just as Dad was getting ready to make the call, a brown truck drove into the parking lot as our drug accuser emerged from the trailer, climbed into the vehicle and left. It happened within a matter of seconds. Now everyone was gone except the snake man. What did this mean? Were we to stay here in this parking lot with no battery? Alone? Until when? Dad was swearing quietly.

Then, fear hurtled to terror. The Toyota that we'd noticed on arrival, and that I assumed had been empty, sidled up along my side of the car. Snake man was in the passenger seat. He motioned for me to roll down my window.

"Impossible," I said loudly through the glass and shook my head. "Our battery is dead." He slithered out of the faded yellow hatchback.

"Open the door. You need our help," he said in English.

Two other men were climbing out of the back behind him. I could not see the driver's face. They all looked disheveled. Had they been waiting there the whole time?

"No. No, thank you. We are fine. Really." I said with a smile and a nod. I glanced at my father. He was frozen.

"No. You need our help. We are going to help you. Open your door." His voice was stern and unflinching.

Oh my god. Had we been thrown to the wolves? No one knew where we were except Rene. I wanted to write a good-bye note to my girls, to talk to them and to my husband. The two men who had gotten out of the back of their car began circling our Honda, limp smiles on their faces. Jackals. I grabbed my father's hand and held tight.

I yelled through the glass and lied. "Someone is coming. Thank you, anyway."

They regarded the car's tires and stood back as if appraising how much they could get for the vehicle. I searched for something to use as a weapon. Then, like a cue from a movie, I heard fast wheels on gravel. Sebastian's cruiser raced straight for us.

He leaped out of his car and walked directly over to the snake man, who lifted his chin in defiance. I tried to make out some words over Dad's wheezing. Sebastian stood firmly, nodding, smiling pleasantly and repeating *gracias*. There they stood, and no one moved. Finally, the snake man called to his companions. They retreated into the Toyota and exited the lot. So these two knew each other? And Sebastian was the good guy? I didn't know what was going on, but I was grateful.

I squeezed my dad's hand and opened the door, wanting to embrace this man who I guessed had just saved us from unimaginable harm. He explained that he had received a phone call from his superior. Rene had come through and gotten law enforcement to reach out. Sebastian would return our original set of keys, jump our car, and lead us to a safe hotel. There would be no trouble. Tomorrow we would rent a car to continue on our way, and the hotel would secure storage for the illegal Honda.

Two days later sitting in a restaurant with Rene, we would learn that we had been very lucky. Men like the guys in the Toyota preyed on hapless travelers like ourselves after the police were done with them.

Before the end of the week, Dad would make it to his doctor's appointment and I would begin writing letters to my husband and girls.

Quest of the Buckwheaters
by Aaron C Palmer

William "Doc" Horton, a.k.a. Donald J. Kramer, was caught hoodwinking investors out of thousands of dollars in various scams. He started by bottling and selling the local sulfur spring water infused with lavender as a cure-all. Using a typical snake oil salesman ploy, he timed it so the townspeople would be talking about the healing waters when investors came to town. He even paid local drunks to praise it as a panacea to alcoholism.

Doc's real intent was to profit by selling property that didn't belong to him. He claimed the land was geographically located in a 'miracle-triangle' where healing waters lay just below the surface. He'd circulated flyers in the business districts of San Francisco and Sacramento showing an illustration resembling the Garden of Eden, but stopped short of calling the spring waters therein, the Fountain of Youth. "Get in on the Health Rush," was emblazoned on the flyers. Doc just needed one quality property he could use to exploit the hungry investors.

Horton might have pulled it off, had he not chosen to con the mother of the local bank president out of her home on forty acres. He claimed her land had "bad" water that needed his special treatment and allegedly poisoned her dog for proof. She was moved to the sanitarium where the good 'Doctor' could administer cures of the healing water for a fee. With fabricated deeds, her property was sold six times, and the neighboring parcels as well. Doc was fixing to leave town when the banker came back from his trip to the city and found his mother in quarantine.

Sheriff Johnston, to whom the banker appealed for justice, was familiar with snake oil salesmen. He'd apprehend them and offer them a choice: leave immediately or be locked up for a week. None were foolish enough to opt for the free room and board. However, Doc Horton's crimes were an advanced level of deceit. Though he was captured with the deposit money on him, the banker wanted Doc hanged. The victims all bemoaned a trial because it meant they would have to come back to town from wherever they'd fled, costing them time and money. Johnston had his own solution.

The early morning sun reflected off the dew-veiled dome of the straw cowboy hat and assembled in dark rivulets that fell past the earnest face of James "Chaps" McCallister. The other man, a reluctant cowboy named Alonzo, or Al, favored a black felt hat, with nary a speck of dust to sully his proud demeanor. They rode up to the jailhouse.

Chaps was worried. "What do ya suppose the sheriff wants?"

Al shrugged. "I told the folks I might be gone a few days."

The young men had spent the last five years causing a rolling ruckus. Herding pigs into the Lutheran church to surprise the Sunday parishioners. "Borrowing" neighbors' horses and racing them until they collapsed. Al, being sweet on a local working girl, nearly beat a 'John' to death, while Chaps held back the brothel's muscle. To the sheriff, their activities better resembled felonies than harmless pranks.

Chaps and Al tied up their steeds and met the sheriff waiting for them leaning against the doorjamb to his office.

The sheriff cleared his throat. "The good people of this town are tired of your shenanigans. So I'm assigning a task that will instill personal accountability and respect for the law."

The lads looked at each other.

"It's time to man-up boys. You're going to escort the grifter out of town, never to return." The sheriff eyed them. "And don't talk to him, he's as slippery as they come."

The men nodded. "We're up for the task, Sheriff," Chaps said.

The sheriff frowned. "You buckwheaters better not let me down. There's always room for a couple more in the hoosegow."

"Yessir," they said in sync.

"Alright, vamoose!"

The men trussed Doc to Nico, Al's cantankerous draft neddy, like an ornery sack of grain. The procession brought much levity to the citizens of Paso Robles along with a chicken coop's amount of eggs thrown at the well-dressed charlatan.

The mid-morning fog of June-gloom hovered over the trail heading west. The aroma of azure lupines hung in the air, and poppies left orange blazes on the hillsides. Late spring was the wondrous time along the central coast of California—the salad month between sneezing season and the mercury cresting dog days of summer.

From his position on his donkey, which followed the two horses, Doc carefully observed the lads and felt he had them reasonably pegged after only a few minutes watching their mannerisms. Additional cold-reading would clarify further details of their personalities.

The barrel-chested Al Martone was blunt-faced and endowed with dark wavy hair and olive skin. What Doc couldn't tell by looking was that he worked the family vineyard and had been making wine since he was twelve. He was the first Martone born in America and intoned a distinct Italian accent conjoined with western jargon.

After the trio had traveled several miles out of town, Al spoke to his childhood friend frankly, and with an equanimity of respect. "I think we oughta off him. There's no reason to waste our time out here." Al didn't care if Doc heard him.

"The sheriff said to do the right thing," replied Chaps. "I don't believe he deserves *that* just yet."

Chaps tightened the grip on Black Star's reigns. Chaps was tall, like his horse, and looked imposing, if not for his ever-present boyish grin. His auburn hair was nearly hidden by his ten-gallon hat. He was the embodiment of the western cowboy, complete with a championship bull-riding belt buckle and Texas drawl being that his father was a San Antonio native.

Al looked over at Doc and shook his head. "He ain't worth the time, is all I'm saying."

"Maybe we'll run into the Shrub, he might have an idea of what to do with him." Chaps grinned. The Shrub was a famous prospector that many had heard of but few had seen. He was said to live by trading with travelers and making lonely strangers put in hard labor to help him extract gold from the land. Everyone half believed this was a fable, but enough people had testified to encountering him that most believed in his existence.

"Momma Mia!" Al shook like he'd gotten the willies. He pulled his *manu cortu* from under his shirt and kissed it. The long masses at the Mission San Miguel Arcángel left him with a certain amount of superstition.

"He's just an old prospector." Chaps was enjoying Al's rattled reaction, as he was usually steady as the afternoon on-shore breeze.

Doc smiled inwardly. It's the little things that irritate, divide, and destroy: a pebble in your boot. The hint of infidelity. Ghosts. The Shrub angle could prove to be their undoing.

Chaps continued, "All Sheriff Johnston said was to make sure this character was never seen again in these parts."

"Into the Scotsman's abandoned mine shaft," Al said, pokerfaced.

"Naw. He just wants us to put the scare to him. Give him a thorough whipping and leave him to his own devices. Besides, I believe the Shrub has laid claim to that mine." Chaps looked for Al's reaction out of the corner of his eye.

Al shook the sweat from his hat. "Enough with the Shrub!" He carefully put his hat on making sure it was straight. "What's your plan?"

"What I reckon, is we get him on the next boat to China."

Al laughed hard. "Just throw a Coolie hat on him, eh?"

"Well..." Chaps glanced at their prisoner, twelve feet of rope between them. "Hey, Doc, you got any ideas?"

Al jumped in before Doc had a chance to answer. "The sheriff said not to talk to him, Chaps. He'd talk you outta Black Star."

"I just wanna see what punishment he thinks he deserves."

Doc cleared his throat. "This ride on your donkey feels like enough. It's busting my back." He groaned.

Chaps could tell by Al's crooked smile that he wasn't buying any of it.

Chaps narrowed his eyes at Doc. "We gotta gets you at least to the next county."

"Or, down the shaft," Al countered, without humor.

Also tied to the donkey was Doc's small leather satchel of personal effects. Of these chattels were: a stethoscope, his wallet, a hairbrush, healing liniments, and miniature bottles of tinctures for objectives only Doc understood.

They rode up through a narrow serpentine rise of slip-rock on the edge of a steep precipice. The horses nickered in complaint, and the donkey, who'd moved to the front and had been acting like the lead "horse" on the ridge made no forward progress.

"Come on Nico!" Chaps coaxed.

"Brutto figlio di puttana bastardo!" Al shook his head at Chaps. "He does this at least once an hour when I plow the vineyard. We will walk this section."

"How about our friend here?"

"Him too, and he's *not* our friend." Al gritted his teeth.

The lads dismounted, and Chaps went over to Nico and untied the "payload."

Horton slipped off the donkey, and fell on his behind, ejecting metamorphic fragments over the escarpment. "God almighty that smarts." He flicked eggshells out of his hair and looked up the barrel of Chaps' shotgun.

"You get on up and get moving," ordered Chaps. "Stay between me and Al. I don't want to have to shoot ye…but I will."

Horton saw an opening, *This one was raised with a conscience.* "I wouldn't be your first, eh?"

Chaps caught a chill. "You'd better just concern yourself with what happens to you, mister."

"But you felt guilt. You don't like killing, do you? Chaps, is it?"

Chaps gestured him to move on with the barrel. "I didn't, it was self—"

"Remember what the sheriff said?" Al boomed.

"I know, he's a sharpie," Chaps said with an edge.

"Then don't talk to the damn palooka!"

"I, I'm a family man," Doc interjected.

"Good for you," Al said with heavy sarcasm.

"You don't say, boys or girls?" Chaps asked.

"I've got one of each, Chaps. They are my pride and joy. It's the only reason I'm out on the road, I'm just trying to provide for them best I can."

"*Gesù Cristo*, can't you see he's trying to goad you into sympathy?" Al spat.

The path veered away from the hillside opening onto a meadow accented with wildflowers of periwinkle and butterscotch. The equines fed on the grasses. The dudes took out their knapsacks and began to eat their sandwiches. Chaps handed Doc half of his own and sat on a rocky outcropping. Al leaned against a blue oak and ate while keeping an eye on Doc Horton the entire time.

Chaps pointed up the trail. "At the top of the ridge, you can see the Pacific coastline on a clear day."

"No kidding?" Doc enthused.

Al shook his head at them. "How much is Doc paying you to be his tour guide?"

Chaps' face turned red.

After finishing his sandwich, Al went over to Chaps and passed him a bottle. He spoke in a low voice. "The shaft is just a mile north from where the trail splits at the top of the range. We could be back home before sundown."

Chaps took a slug, scowled at Al, and took another. He glanced over at their prisoner enjoying his sandwich. "I don't believe that's necessary. He's no worse than us, and he has a family depending on him."

Al took the bottle back and drank. "*Paisano*, you don't know that. We don't know nuthin' about that guy. And the sheriff said we could do what we want, as long as he never sees the scoundrel again. Dropping him headfirst down that mine shaft will ensure he ain't coming back."

Taking the bottle, Chaps shook his head and frowned. "I'm not comfortable being his judge and jury, I mean if he came at us, or stole from my kin, I could see it—"

"I'll kill him. You can stay pure this time, good buddy."

"Now Al, that's even worse. You's saying I don't have the guts?"

"I'm calling a spade a spade, cowboy. You watch that guy, I gotta feed some bears." Al went into the woods looking for privacy.

Doc smiled at Chaps. "I appreciate the grub. I was near starvation. Can I trouble you for some water?"

Chaps nodded and brought him his canteen.

Doc took a long drink. "You're a compassionate captor." Doc smiled. "Ya think I could get a taste of that elixir?"

Chaps thought about what Al said, but gave in. "Just a sip."

Doc took a swig and turned away briefly, while Chaps wet his bandanna with water and wiped his mouth and brow.

Doc handed the whiskey back. "You suppose we'll see the Shrub? I've heard stories of him way up in Sacramento."

"Don't reckon I'd know. My pops said people'd spot him out here before the war, but I ain't never seen him."

"Seems like a peaceful existence, living alone among God's bounty."

Chaps nodded. "I'd miss the womenfolk too much."

Doc felt Chaps was a veritable sponge now. "I could do it. God is everywhere out here. A fine place to get oneself pure again."

"Al doesn't much change his mind. If he means to off you, that's it."

"Well you're partners, right? He's got to take your side into account. And I think I know how you feel. You have a job to do, but you're not real comfortable with Al's solution." Doc gazed solemnly toward the heavens. "Sometimes you need to stand up for what's right."

Doc looked at Chaps as though he could see into his mind. Chaps appeared wary and hesitant. He didn't want to get taken, but he wanted to believe Doc was repentant and of the genuine sort. Alluding to do what's right in the eyes of the Lord touched Chaps. It was something a corn-fed boy, raised with biblical teachings could not run from.

Chaps took another large swallow. He stared at Doc.

"I believe most fellas deserve a second chance. What would you do if we let you go?"

Doc's eyes welled, and he looked up at Chaps. "Why, I would find Jesus in my heart. I'd go home to my family and hug them like no tomorrow. Then, I'd read, and live by the teaching of the good book. I'd find honest work and pay back those I bilked." His chin wobbled as he spoke. *He was good.*

Chaps nodded. "I reckon, that's about the best a man could do."

Doc looked up meekly. "I just want to say how much I appreciate your humanity."

"What's he sayin'?" Al grumbled, coming into view.

"Nuthin'. It's my turn." Chaps handed him the whiskey and hobbled into the woods.

Doc gave an obsequious smile. "Your buddy's got quite the limp. Rodeo?" Doc asked.

"You could say that," Al said evenly finishing the bottle.

Doc used his dramatic skills by appearing small and submissive. He said with a hitch in his voice, "Mr. Martone, you may not like me. You may not trust me, but I see grace in you."

Al gave him a dead-eyed glare. "Why would I believe a word you say?"

Doc made himself appear embarrassed. His face flushed, and he looked down at his dusty alligator-skin boots. "I can tell you're the leader, the brainy one of the two." He opened his hands in surrender. "Not to say your friend ain't got smarts. But you, you see it all. You're always a step ahead. Your calling will be bigger than what a small country town can give you." Doc watched Al begin to puff up.

Suddenly, the sound of approaching steps and Al readied his rifle. When the stranger came into view, Al's eyes grew large with surprise. He was stricken paralytic.

"Howdy, partner," the little man said. "They call me the Shrub." He did a little jig and took a bow. The nomad talked with a country brogue which gave a stammering rhythm to his cadence.

Doc considered the scene, and grinned, but kept his mouth shut. Shrub was wiry, and maybe five feet tall. He was crusted with trail dust, and wooly, silver hair grew out from nearly every part of his head. He walked beside a grey-muzzled pack mule loaded with a prospector's kit: a pick and shovel, kindling hatchet, a blanket roll, one blackened pot, a folded oil cloth tarp, and a coil of frayed hemp rope.

Al snapped back into focus. He moved aside, and gestured for Shrub to carry on, but Shrub didn't move.

"I see you got yourselves a prisoner…how much you want for him?" He walked over to Doc, who had an unlit pipe in his mouth. Shrub flicked his thumb up, and a flame appeared. A parlor trick.

Doc puffed on his pipe. "Much appreciated," he said, smiling through the smoke.

Al was stunned into silence and didn't hear Chaps beside him. When Chaps slapped his back, Al jumped.

"What have we got here?" Chaps said with a toothy grin.

"It's the Shrub," Al said. "He's offering to buy Doc from us."

Chaps walked over and shook the Shrub's diminutive hand. "Hey there, I'm Chaps." He looked like a giant next to the wee man. "What kinda deal you got in mind?"

The Shrub looked at Chaps with a twinkle in his eyes. "I could use some digging help at my claims and this here fella looks like he could swing a pick."

Doc wrinkled his brow.

"What's your payment?" Al asked.

Shrub gave a lecherous smirk. "I figure I'm doing you boys a favor. I don't come along without first hearing the call—"

"What're you saying?" Al narrowed his eyes.

"I think he's offering to help," Chaps said.

Shrub smiled, showing only a handful of teeth. "Amen."

Al pointed at Doc. "What's to keep him from taking the pick to your head?"

"I know a kindred spirit when I see one," Shrub replied.

"I don't know. If that scoundrel ends up back in town, the sheriff's gonna lock us all up." Al said with an edge.

Chaps groaned.

The Shrub pulled out a small, blackened silk bag and untied it. "I figured you's might need a little coaxing." He pulled out two grape-sized, oblong stream polished nuggets. "These weigh 'bout the same."

The boys' eyes grew large. Doc continued to puff away on his pipe. Shrub put one in Al's and Chaps' hands. They had never felt real gold before.

"Lotta weight for a little thing," Chaps conceded.

The Shrub chuckled. "Oh, that ain't nothin' compared to what I'd get in the Sierras. Big though, for these parts."

Chaps held up his nugget in the sunlight until Al elbowed him.

"We gots to talk this out," Al said.

Chaps followed him just out of earshot. "What's your take?"

"Lemme see yours." Al weighed them in each hand and nodded. Then he bit down on his and looked at the indentation. "Seems to be the real McCoy."

"Let's do it then."

The friends walked back trying to hold in their smiles. Then froze in their steps. Only the donkey was accounted for.

"God almighty, they done taken our mounts!" Chaps threw down his hat.

Al's face burned with anger. "*Merda.*"

Chaps grimaced.

"We will tell no one about this. No one!" Al spat.

"Agreed." Chaps pushed his hat back.

"I need momma's lasagna." Al mumbled to himself.

"Al?"

"Yeah, cowboy."

"You were right. We shoulda thrown him down the shaft."

All about Tristan
by Kathy Wagner

That first Wednesday, I worked from a coffee shop just a few blocks from The Door. Not that I got much work done, but I didn't want to worry about traffic or being late to go see Tristan. As afternoon rolled toward evening, I gave up even pretending to be productive.

I watched people pass by on the sidewalk. Businesspeople, homeless people, students. I checked the time—5:07—and sighed.

There was a minor commotion out front and, for a moment, I was confused by the jumble of metal, purple floral print, and glass before I realized an elderly lady in a walker was struggling to open the glass door. I jumped off my stool and held the door for her. I hoped I hadn't been gawking for too long.

She thanked me and I smiled.

By the time I was back in my seat and checked the time again, it was 5:12. Time to put my mind to answering the question that had been rattling in my head all day: Would

Tristan prefer I bring him a strawberry Frappuccino or a vanilla one? I knew he'd be happy with either. Nobody was more exuberant about food than Tristan. I could put anything edible in front of him and he was like a puppy with a bowl of ice cream. But I also knew that he'd *prefer* one over the other depending on his mood. And I had no way of knowing if he was in a strawberry mood or a vanilla mood.

I was trying to remember how many times I'd seen Tristan order one of those flavors compared to the other, when my phone rang.

It was The Door. I had no idea why they'd call me now, an hour before I was due to arrive there for my first meeting with Tristan, and then my first Parents Group. My heart was pounding as I answered, "Hello?"

"Hi Kathy, I'm just phoning to give you an update. Everything's fine and there's no reason to worry." It was Ben, Tristan's caseworker. He'd called a few times over the past week and began every conversation this way. "But Tristan had a bad day, so he won't be able to visit with you this evening."

A thud landed heavy in my stomach. I didn't know what a bad day might look like for Tristan now. No idea. Was it a bad case of the blues? Did he want to run away and give up? Did he punch someone? Did he go all crazy and psychotic?

"What happened?" I asked.

"Oh, he was butting heads with our director at dinner tonight. Dale called him out on his table manners, and Tristan started mouthing off. That's not unusual for new guys," he reassured me. "They rebel against authority and don't like to follow rules. I know, I was the same way. And then they just get stuck in the anger, haven't got a good range of emotions yet. I don't know if you've met Dale, but the guys don't get away with too much around him. He calls them on their bullshit."

I had met Dale, briefly. A beefy, middle-aged biker-looking dude with sharp eyes, a foul mouth, and plaid flannel covering a generous heart. But something didn't seem right in what Ben was telling me. Tristan looked up to men in authority, showed them respect, even awe. He was a follower, not a leader, always on the lookout for male role models. I'd have thought he would have tried hard to stay on Dale's good side.

"Well...what happened?" I still didn't get it, clearly.

"It's all good now. Tristan took it hard and wanted to walk out, but the guys talked to him and he had a bit of a cry in his room and then found Dale and apologized. They hugged it out, no hard feelings. Tristan just needs to learn when it's best to stay quiet. He says he's still committed to being here, but I think it's best if he has a calm evening with the guys and we try again next week for a visit with you. But you're still coming to Parents Group?"

"Yes, of course. Thanks for..." my thoughts wandered off. I didn't really know what I was thanking him for. "For letting me know," I finished.

"No problem. I'll see you soon."

I sat and stared out the window. I was deeply disappointed in not being able to see Tristan after twelve days of no communication. I'd been looking forward to that precious half hour with him much more than the weekly Parents Group they ran at his center. Now I was stuck with the chaff of the evening, without the wheat. I blinked back tears and sipped my cold tea to steady myself.

My mind whirred over what Ben had said. Something was wrong. Tristan, *my* Tristan, didn't talk back to men in authority. He might have muttered under his breath, but I couldn't see him going head to head with Dale. And Tristan needed to learn how to stay quiet? Tristan was the epitome of repressed feelings and lack of expression. He lived in his head and second-guessed every word that came out of his mouth, usually before they did. He needed to learn to speak up, not stay quiet. Was The Door paying any attention to Tristan's sweet soul? Did they even see him?

It made no sense to me that The Door hadn't asked for my opinion about how to treat Tristan. Who knew my son better than I did? They didn't know what he would respond well to, and what he wouldn't. They didn't know what made him tick like I did. They talked about including family in addiction recovery, but maybe that was just lip service to reassure me. Sure, they offered group sessions for parents and siblings, and another for spouses and children, but how did that help an addict's recovery? They certainly weren't using me as a resource to help them understand Tristan.

It didn't seem like a good start, to me.

I was still frazzled and anxious as I drove to Parents Group. I tried to calm myself and focus on the experience in front of me. There was still so much I could learn about Tristan's environment, even if I couldn't see him tonight. And if Ben said that Tristan was fine, even with the drama of the evening— that mood swings and conflict at this stage of recovery were normal, even—then I needed to try to believe that.

I'd had a tour of The Last Door—or, more simply, "The Door"—when I dropped Tristan off, so I knew where I was going. The whole center was spread across three buildings: two low-rise apartment buildings and one large heritage home on a typical suburban street. Nothing fancy, but clean, comfortable, homey. Parents Group took place in the back room of the heritage house, and at 6:57, with three minutes to spare, I walked up the front stairs.

This is where Tristan lives now, I thought.

One of the residents saw me, opened the door, and said hi. I said hi back as I scanned the living room for Tristan, knowing I wouldn't see him. There were some guys playing chess, another strumming a guitar, a few writing in notebooks, and a bunch just standing around talking. I was reassured by the huge bowl of apples, oranges, and bananas that sat on a side table. Nobody was starving here. There was an abundance of tattoos, but everybody looked healthy and happy. Just regular guys.

But no Tristan.

I walked through the kitchen and into the multipurpose room where they held the meetings. I had timed my entrance carefully. Not so late as to draw attention to myself, but not so early that I'd have to make conversation. I quickly sat in the first empty chair I saw and smiled and nodded at whoever looked my way, to be friendly. Then I avoided further contact by pretending that I had urgent messages to answer on my phone.

Talking with strangers wasn't easy for me and being in large groups of people made me anxious. But I would have endured any nightmare to get a glimpse into Tristan's new world.

There were about twenty or so parents, mostly women, mostly middle-aged, sitting on stackable chairs set in a circle around the perimeter of the room. Their laughter and camaraderie, the easy flow of conversation, was unfamiliar to me. I felt out of place.

Stacks of more chairs stood against the back wall, along with folding tables that would be set out at breakfast, lunch, and dinner.

This is where Tristan eats his meals.

There were two huge chalkboards at each end of the room. Scrawled on one chalkboard were ten characteristics of low self-esteem. The other chalkboard listed characteristics of high self-esteem. The low esteem board described Tristan pretty accurately, I thought—extremely self-critical, needing affirmation from other people. For myself, I had more high self-esteem characteristics than low and felt oddly proud—like I got a good grade on a test. Not an A, but a C+ at least, maybe a B.

This is where Tristan attends group meetings.

Ben came in and sat in front of the low self-esteem board. It was the first time that I'd seen him since he'd shown me around during Tristan's intake. He was in his late twenties, stocky build, buzz-cut hair. He saw me and waved hello as he continued talking to the woman next to him.

Tristan's caseworker.

Another guy came in and sat in front of the high self-esteem board. He seemed ageless. He was dressed like a teenager: jeans, a rumpled button-down shirt, and sneakers. His face was neither young nor old, but clearly had experience.

He said hello to the group and introduced himself because there were a few of us first-time parents that night. His name was Paul. He was the lead facilitator of the Parents Group and head counselor for the youth program. That fit perfectly. Teenagers would feel right at home with him. He looked like one of them, but older.

I had expected to hear an overview of how these sessions worked, but Paul jumped right in with a story about his background and path to recovery.

"I told myself I had every reason to use," Paul said. "My parents died when I was young, and I'd been in the foster system before I was adopted. Poor me. I was angry at the world, I fought, I stole, I lied to get drugs. I was the neighborhood punk that everyone stayed away from. One day, I went home and my key didn't work. My parents had changed the locks. I pounded on the door until my dad came down and told me he was tired of me upsetting my mom, and if he saw me around their house again, he'd call the cops. *Their* house, not mine. The nerve, right?" Paul's smile was at odds with the tragedy of his story, like he found his younger self highly entertaining. Then, he began flat-out laughing at himself.

"I was like, 'Whatever, I don't need you or your stupid home!' and I stomped halfway down the block before realizing it was cold and I had nowhere to go. I felt like such a big tough guy, but I turned around and went back to the house and started yelling, 'Mom! Mommy, Mommy I want my blanket!' Seriously, I was nineteen years old and yelling for 'mommy' to get my blankey. No joke. So finally, I leave, satisfied, with my favorite Snoopy blanket in hand." Everyone in the room was laughing now, me included. The scene was so familiar. It almost hurt to laugh that hard.

"I couch surfed with friends for a few nights," he continued, "checked out a homeless shelter, and decided I really liked being warm and comfortable. I wouldn't make a good street person. So, I decided to get help. And I came to The Door. That was twenty-six years ago."

Twenty-six years. It was hard to imagine. Proof that recovery was possible. And that Paul was in his mid-forties.

This is Tristan's role model.

There was no real structure to the meeting I could follow, that first time. After Paul spoke for a while, one of the women mentioned that her son celebrated his one-year cake last week, and another that she helped her son and another "Door boy" who had just transitioned out to set up their new apartment. A discussion ensued about when to help and when to step back. Everyone in that room knew it was a tricky tightrope to walk.

"What works for me," said one woman, "is asking myself whether what I'm doing is a *handout*, something that he should be doing for himself, or is it a *hand up*? We still want to help our children when they need it. For example, when Stu was six months out of The Door, he asked us if we'd lend him money so he could buy a car and we said no way. He could save up for one himself. And he did, and he was really proud of that beater." She looked like a proud mama who had set her limits and stuck to them. "Now," she continued, "two years later, he asked us if we'd co-sign on financing so he could get a new truck. He loves to go off-roading and helps a lot of people in recovery to move and pick up furniture. He's been responsible with managing his money and making payments, so we said sure. Buying a car for him when he first got out of The Door would have been a handout. Helping him to finance a truck now feels like a hand up."

There were more stories and laughter about boys and their beater cars. I was starting to relax. Starting to see that our kids can get better. That maybe Tristan could get well, move out with a roommate, have a one-year cake, manage his money, and buy a beater car one day. As impossible as that seemed to me right now.

And then a woman across the room mentioned that she'd just got back from what she called "a few days of radical self-care" at her cabin. That she was coping and focusing on her own health and well-being, even though her son had recently relapsed.

Relapsed.

Relapsed.

I couldn't hear what came next. My heart raced. I started to panic.

I wasn't stupid, I knew about relapse. That it was always a possibility. Some say a probability, until a person hits that seemingly magical moment when recovery sticks. *If* they hit that moment. Which, they don't always.

Jesus fucking Christ, Tristan can't relapse. I do not have another round of this in me. I would rather die.

My fear became visceral and tears blurred my vision. These thoughts didn't feel dramatic to me. They were not an overreaction or exaggeration. They came from a place of deep exhaustion and certainty that I wouldn't have the strength to live through Tristan's addiction again.

My faith in recovery wavered as I watched this woman across from me, so strong and calm, talking about the joy and gratitude she found in hiking and spending time with her husband this past weekend. Despite everything. Despite relapse.

I studied her, like she was a bizarre creature I'd never seen before. Like I wasn't sure if she was dangerous or not. I didn't recognize what I was seeing. I didn't recognize recovery in action—a *mother's* recovery. At that time, recovery wasn't a concept that I applied to myself, or to other parents. Recovery was for our kids, not us. A kid in relapse was a failure, worth screaming about, and grieving, and shrieking, and tearing yourself apart. Did this woman not understand the risks of relapse? Did she not see how quickly people lose themselves in addiction, sometimes forever? How could she possibly go off and enjoy herself, when she should have been chasing her son and tying him up if she had to, to get him back into treatment? And if that wasn't possible, at least she could be in deep despair.

I decided this woman wasn't like me. She had a cabin. And a husband. She felt joy. She had a son who relapsed, and she still felt joy. Clearly, she was nothing like me. This was a good thing, because if she was different, then our sons must be different, and Tristan wouldn't relapse like her son did. I knew my logic was faulty, but it was comforting, and I began to calm down and breathe again.

Part of me registered this woman's son was no longer at The Door, but she kept coming to Parents Group anyway. She was here for herself, not her son. That idea challenged me, and I pushed it away.

Paul closed the meeting after a fast ninety minutes, by reminding us that we "didn't cause it, can't control it, and can't cure it. If you could have, God knows you would have by now."

Everyone stood up, formed a big circle with arms across each other's shoulder, and said the serenity prayer together. I'd heard it before but didn't know the words. It all seemed a bit awkward and churchy, so I was surprised by the surge of emotion that washed over me as I listened. Even if I had known the words, I wouldn't have been able to speak them right then.

As I walked out of the house, many of the parents were mingling with their boys on the open patio outside. They looked happy, parents and boys alike. Some of the "boys" were well into their thirties and forties.

I missed Tristan. I wondered where he was, somewhere in one of these buildings. What was he doing? How was he feeling?

Driving home, I thought about the evening. If someone had asked me then what I had hoped to get out of attending Parents Group, and if I had answered honestly, it would have been all about Tristan. I knew that Parents Group was supposed to be for us, the parents, but I couldn't separate my goals from Tristan. I wanted to learn how to be better, a better parent, *for Tristan.* I wanted to learn how to take better care of myself, so that I could take better care *of Tristan.* I wanted to learn how to have a more fulfilling life, so that I could be a good role model *for Tristan.* Surely, there was nothing wrong with that.

I didn't know yet that my own life was waiting for me beyond Tristan's addiction and recovery. I hadn't clued into The Door's notion that including family in recovery meant helping the whole family to heal themselves, not each other. And I certainly didn't know what a close friend and inspiration that mom in Parents Group would become for me—the woman so unlike me that she fought for her own precious moments of joy, even while her son was in crisis.

All I could see as I unknowingly took that first step into my own recovery, was that nobody else understood how much Tristan needed me. And I had to be there for him.

As I pulled into my driveway that evening, I wasn't sure I'd get anything of value from the Parents Group, but decided I'd go a few more times, at least.

You never know. Maybe I'd get to see Tristan next week.

Desert Daughter
by M. F. Webb

Trains

I snuggle into crisp, white cotton sheets, fragrant with the scent of a sachet from France whose contents I will never be able to determine, which also wafts from the shelves of the old armoire next to the bed. Bars of yellow light slip through the wide Venetian blinds from the streetlight down the sidewalk and fall across the pink chenille bedspread. As I burrow into the feather pillow, I hear the faint whistle of a train approaching and then the rumble of the boxcars. My grandparents' little white house would be right by the railroad tracks if the gravel alleyway and some greasewood bushes didn't separate them. We like to watch the trains when they travel by during the day, and we always watch for the caboose. Sometimes a man is sitting at the back door of the caboose with its little railing, and he waves back to us.

It's a special treat to spend the night here, and not just because of the pretty black iron bed frame in the front room or the Kentucky Fried Chicken we have for dinner. There are books here that I don't have at home, and copies of *Reader's Digest* with lots of jokes in them. A canvas bag of wooden blocks gives me everything I need to build bridges and roads for the orange toy truck that carries a lime green car and a bright pink one on its back.

Sometimes Grandpa pulls me into his lap and tries to get me to stay still for a cuddle. Mostly I giggle and squirm, and he laughs. The smell of the smoke from his pipe is musty and sweet.

After Grandpa dies, "spending the night with Grandmommy" is every Saturday night.

The house is quieter without Grandpa there and I miss the smell of his pipe. But the sachet still saturates the crisp white sheets, and I still hear the trains in the night. I write poems now, and little stories like Carl Sandburg did. I like to describe the moon and the clouds and the night.

In the morning, Grandmommy helps me make the bed. We throw the pillows back and forth to each other until they are fat and almost completely round—a silly game that makes us laugh. Then we have a breakfast of fried eggs and bacon before we get dressed for church. Great-Aunt Mary and Great-Uncle Lewis drive us there in their old blue car. Uncle Lewis is an elder and does something important at the church, so we always go early, and I roam around the building while I wait for the other kids to show up for Sunday school. After church is Sunday dinner, either at my house or Grandmommy's. I'd rather have dinner at Grandmommy's. It means I'm away from our dogs longer, but she doesn't cook dry, awful pork chops for

Sunday dinner the way my mom does. Besides, it can be lonely at my house and I feel like I'm always in trouble.

I play a game with the trains sometimes if I'm in Grand-mommy's yard when I hear one coming. I wait till I catch my first glimpse of the locomotive, then I run and hide behind the car as if the train is chasing me. The engine is always deafen-ingly loud, and I hold my hands against my ears till the train is almost past, when I pop out to see the caboose.

One night a business at a nearby strip shopping center shines a searchlight up against the clouds. It's probably an advertisement for something, but it looks just like a UFO. Even after I figure out what it really is, it's fun to pretend it's circling in preparation for landing and I'd better hide quick.

There's a crawlspace under the house that I've always wanted to see inside, even though Grandmommy says there's nothing there but the heater for the house and dust and spi-ders. No one goes under there except my dad when he's checking the heater, and I'm afraid if I go in when he's around, he'll lock me in because he thinks it's funny. I know he'd let me out, but I hate it when he laughs at me.

I'm a junior in high school now, but I still spend Saturday nights with Grandmommy, even though she encourages me to stay at my own house sometimes so I can see my friends on the weekends. It's usually not worth arguing with my parents about changing their schedule just so I can go on a date or out somewhere with the other drama kids. Grandmommy and I still go to church, but now I drive her in the blue 1972 Mercu-ry that belonged to Grandpa before he died. I'm not allowed to drive on the freeway. I don't know how my dad would know if I did, but I wouldn't put it past him to check the odometer and somehow figure it out. So, I take the long way down Mesa Street and then Montana, past the strip shopping centers and through the residential streets.

I sleep in the other bedroom now, the one with the adjacent half bath and the wooden bed frame. I don't think anyone goes in the front room much now, and the oval mirror over the dresser is dusty. Grandmommy sleeps in the middle bedroom and we call back and forth to each other at bedtime. "Good night. Sleep tight. Don't let the bedbugs bite!" The rest of our exchange may be original to us. "If they do, hit 'em with a shoe. Till they're black and blue!"

I make the bed by myself in the morning. There isn't room on the far side of this bed for us to toss the pillows back and forth, and I think Grandmommy's arthritis might keep her from doing so anyway.

We eat in the back room with the window that looks out into the backyard, with its peach trees and vegetable garden, and then across the dirt alley to the dip where the trains run through. After someone left a puppy in her yard one night, she had a wire fence put up to keep her new dog from escaping. You can still see through the fence as though it weren't there, to the scrub plants and the mesquite tree that one year was hung with glistening icicles after a freak winter storm, the kind you rarely see in El Paso. One of the peach trees has died, and the grass has been worn away by Missy the dog. Missy sometimes seems to love my dad the most, judging from the way she yowls and jumps on him when he stops by, but she's good company for Grandmommy, and she's a nice dog.

The trains are longer every year, with twice as many boxcars as they used to have. Grandmommy and I sit at the back table with our elbows on the red and white checked oilcloth, and we watch them roll by and shout at each other over the noise until they're gone, hauling their cargo wherever they're asked to go, barreling into the distance like a dream you forget as soon as you wake up. It feels like it takes forever now to see the caboose, and these days no one sits behind its little rail waving.

Records

A new vinyl record slides cool from its paper sleeve, crackling with static, rainbows glinting deep within its grooves. It settles down on the stereo spindle, suspended in anticipation before the needle drops—if it lands precisely at the beginning of the first track, the moment will be perfect. The music begins and the world expands.

I discovered this moment of revelation when I was eleven, after a chance viewing on a summer Saturday afternoon of the animated *Yellow Submarine* movie on television. It had probably been broadcast every year for a decade, but suddenly the Beatles were no longer background music to me. They were clever and colorful and real, emissaries from a world of freedom and irreverence I craved. Ringo was my intended boyfriend, the melancholy soul who needed someone to love and care for him, but I suspected my own persona was more that of John.

And then John Lennon was murdered, and my view of the larger world shifted into a more fraught and fragile state. The Beatles seemed at once more vital and more vulnerable, real people who could be hurt, not just images on a screen or voices on vinyl. I was spun further into my infatuation, and the foursome displaced the poems about fairies and mermaids I'd once written, filling my imagination with their own music and adventures.

I had one friend whom I trusted with the depth of my earnest affection for the Beatles. My classmates at parochial school had already proven themselves eager to use every evidence of anything I cared about as a cudgel. But Anna, a friend I met when we both brought new puppies to a Girl Scout dog obedience class, shared my musical ardor, though her fondness for Olivia Newton-John may not have resembled my Beatlemania point for point. My mother would drop me off at her house, where we would compare the covers and title notes on my newest record album with those on her most recent acquisition. Then, of course, we listened to both albums. Going to Anna's house was better than spending time in mine, because she could play her records on the family stereo—something I wasn't allowed to do at my own house.

My parents' big stereo was housed in a long console that took up one wall in the living room, off-limits unless they were out. I lived for the afternoons when they left me alone for an hour or more. Carefully I would slide away the console cover, breathe in the fragrance of furniture wax and the row of albums by Mantovani and other masters of easy listening, and set my own record gently upon the spindle. I could play it as loudly as I wanted, as long as there was silence when my parents returned home.

If a particular subset of films had existed then, about teenagers finding the solace and understanding they need in music—*Sing Street, Blinded by the Light*—I might have felt less alone in my obsession. Instead, music became something which estranged me further from my family. I wasn't forbidden to listen to my music, but I was discouraged in every way from making it other than a solitary pastime. I could paper my bedroom walls with Beatles photographs, but I was only allowed to play their music softly on my little suitcase-style record player with my bedroom door closed.

Rock concerts were forbidden to me, along with R-rated movies, Monty Python, and *Saturday Night Live*. Not knowing this, Anna gave me a ticket to a Beatles cover concert for my thirteenth birthday. Her mother would go with us to a small safe venue. But my father said no, and my mother took his side.

Entry upon entry in the journal I kept that year recounts screaming fights that ensued for days, a scene paralleled in the movie *Blinded by the Light* when the protagonist wants to see his hero Bruce Springsteen in concert. I did not get to see the Beatles cover band, that year or any other. If I had known of any other child in the world who'd had that experience, I'm certain I would have felt less desperately alone.

Still, I had inherited my father's stubbornness, and I didn't stop caring about the Beatles, or the music I discovered in later years.

My middle school classmates admitted to liking only heavy metal, and the soundtrack to high school was radio pop. El Paso in the 1980s was not an easy place to discover alternative music. But MTV brought me Siouxsie and the Banshees and Bronski Beat, and a few students from drama class introduced me to assorted new wave musicians. A new and exhilarating world of music lay beyond my former experience, another existence opening up beyond the one I wished to escape.

I fell into conversation with a local DJ at a record show my senior year of high school, and he offered me a job working at his record store my first summer home from college. My father didn't openly object, but the night I stayed late to help with inventory, he phoned every half hour to check on me, to my embarrassment and the frustration of the rest of the staff.

Not only was I surrounded at the record store by music and people who loved it as much as I did, but the DJ let me order single copies of albums from the shop catalogs for myself. Voraciously I explored the listings, and there I discovered the artists who were to pull me through difficult days in my small, conservative Texas university—Kate Bush, The Cure, anything from the 4AD record label, working-class British bands who were as distressed by the state of the world under Ronald Reagan and Margaret Thatcher as I was. I found only a few fellow travelers in college, but there was comfort in knowing that a world of like-minded music fans existed, and someday I might find my way to them. My second month in college, I finally went to my first rock concert: Tears for Fears at the Dallas Convention Center.

My father never gave my music much of a chance. Since he seemed to have become culturally stuck in 1963, it was perhaps inevitable that I would try to pull him into subsequent generations—and perhaps equally likely that I would fail. For years I played him songs I thought he might like. "He's either a talented pianist or very well trained," he sniffed of Style Council. "Probably very well trained." We eventually compromised on "smooth jazz" for the car, but this was not something I sought out on my own. Music remained one of the many fields on which we would never peacefully meet.

Today I own a high-end turntable. My hundreds of college cassette tapes gave way to an equally overwhelming number of CDs, and I've rediscovered vinyl. I have spent far more nights in noisy clubs and loud concert venues than my parents would ever care to know, and I have the tinnitus to prove it. Yet I wonder how my music would sound now were I to listen to it alone in my parents' house on their enormous stereo console, either something recently discovered or a Beatles album from the year I was twelve. Would the melody envelope me with the solace and thrill I remember, that promise of companionship and future adventure? Or was this youthful experience an incidence of transient grace, something that I would have shared if I'd been able, but which was always fated to be mine alone?

Garden Hose

Water in the desert is a trick. Its rain is brief and half-hearted, or sudden and torrential. The shimmer in the distance that must surely be a lake, even one alkaline and undrinkable, is nothing more than refracted light. The river that once inspired the name of "Grande" is a sheen of dampness along a depression of cracked mud, its bounty now trapped by a dam in another state. There are two hundred days of sunshine in El Paso, Texas, every year, and it wilts everything beneath it.

The child you were lived in anticipation of rain. Rain in El Paso was a breath of coolness in a thirsty season, a tumult of scarlet bird-of-paradise blooming at the bottom of an arroyo that otherwise was a crumbled valley of rock and yucca, prickly pear and creosote. Rain was often the only beauty you could find in a parched and pallid landscape.

Thunderstorms were best, their lightning snaking through the sky or trembling against the horizon, petrichor seeping up from the baked sidewalk like the smell of nourishing soil. But even a sprinkle delighted you. At six years old, you eagerly listened for the growl of thunder every summer afternoon. You scurried outside when the rain began with a red-haired doll the size of your hand from the *mercado* in Juárez, a companion dressed in a blue and green floral raincoat and matching hat. And you even had your own umbrella, clear plastic spattered with large polka dots, but not so many that you couldn't see the dark clouds massed overhead.

Surely your father did not realize, the first time he trained the garden hose on your bedroom window, how delighted you would be. He didn't know how something inside you bloomed in the misty rain when you visited family in Vancouver, B.C., or when you first saw Puget Sound from the deck of the Space Needle in Seattle when you were ten, fighting your fear of heights because that view of salt water was more important than fear.

But your glee sparked something similar in him. You and your father played this peekaboo garden hose game even into your teens, even when you could barely be in a room together without fighting. And even then, you sometimes pretended you were hearing a sudden burst of rain against your window.

You know now that beauty can be found in the west Texas desert. Your grandmother painted it in oils of pale blue and olive green and tan, a low purple mountain along the horizon. You see it in other people's photos: Transmountain Road at night, lights spilling out beyond it to the horizon, picking out the streets and neighborhoods that extend from El Paso to *Ciudad Juárez*. You yourself have captured the image of a block of gray rainclouds moving toward the end of a half-finished street at the edge of town, slowly enough to be photographed before you had to run for shelter.

The open sky and bright landscape of the far West Texas desert can look as though the entire world has been scrubbed clean, even when you know that the truth is smokestacks and industrial waste. Even though your birthday in March was marked every year by fifty-mile-per-hour winds that shrouded the city in dust, clouds of fine grit so concentrated they can hide a small mountain even when you live on its foothills. These storms can last hours and repeat for days, forcing powdered sand under door frames and into noses and eyes, around the items heaped in locked outdoor storage units.

Not all desert is West Texas, of course. Visiting New Mexico two years ago, you'd forgotten how rapidly the landscape changes as a car crosses the state line, how pale caliche soil gives way to sweeps of muted sepia and ochre-tinged green as you draw nearer the craggy Organ Mountains. How the sky opens up to promise a deep breath of clarity and not merely a gasp for air. How the distant scrub and mesquite and rocks (always so many rocks) are transmuted to the softness of an oil painting as you speed past them.

You have now seen the red sands of Utah desert, the terrifying splendor of the Grand Canyon and Zion National Park. The many-armed saguaro cacti standing sentinel in the Arizona desert, purple shadows on coral-colored sand, rock formations scoured by the winds of centuries. Sky and sand holding sunset colors close in the late afternoon and the traces of animal tracks revealed by lengthening light. You know that the desert is beautiful in its own right.

But in your mind, El Paso is the wasteland your military friend compared to Afghanistan, scorched and dusty, drab and forlorn. It is faded soil and plants that can only survive by growing daggers and thorns. It is water only provided sporadically and with possible danger. It is water only predictable from a garden hose.

When you were a child, every form of weather aside from a sunny day let you imagine you were somewhere else. A crisp morning near the end of autumn could be in Canada, or Fairyland. A rainy day might be England, or somewhere near the ocean where grass grew green of its own accord and wasn't transplanted from elsewhere and coaxed to stay alive. Rain fed more than the transplanted trees around you and the throttled river that tried to sustain them.

You live now, at last, in a rainy place. Even after the months of gray winter overcast that constitute winters here, you can't quite celebrate a cloudless day. "I didn't move from Texas to the Pacific Northwest for sunshine," you joke. You keep to yourself the apprehension that too much sunshine will become the lack of everything that nourishes.

You can see the grandeur and beauty of the American Southwest, and these feed a wide and echoing part of you as well.

But you cannot live in the desert again.

Appalachian Yankees
by Wendy Welch

Call us Appalachian Yankees. My family has spent three generations driving up and down I-75 looking for work someplace between Michigan and Tennessee.

That's not the only road some of us have tried to leave. Working class folk descended from mountain Christianity with a capital C: that's my people. When you look up fundamentalist in the dictionary, you find a picture of Grandma Mattie. In 1937, she and Grandpa Alex abandoned a crossroads general store in Tazewell, Tennessee, for a slum-burb in Detroit, where he became a bricklayer and she raised five children.

The Tazewell church they never left behind didn't hold with adornment: no curling of the hair, no wedding rings, not even reading glasses. If God hadn't equipped you with it when you came out of the womb, you didn't need it. No good ever came of reading too much anyway. The purpose of life was to glorify God and take good care of your family. This is our creed.

Three out of four aunts agreed, but Aunt Lelah struck out sideways, settling in rural Ohio with a Navy man. No one can explain why this loosened her up a bit, but theirs was the first daughter to show up at the annual Christmas gathering in blue jeans. Scandalized glances fell aplenty, but family is family. In later years two sisters and a brother used Lelah's house as a stopover *en route* to destinies of their own as teacher, nurse, and preacher back in the region Mattie and Alex had left the generation before.

We cousins retraced Grandma and Grandpa's route back and forth, spreading out into Chicago and a few other off-shoots of the I-75 corridor, aiming at ever-moving targets of jobs and theology. Sometimes steel mills and college classes proved infertile soil for Tazewell's brand of Christianity. Some cousins raced through life well above the speed limit aided by an excess of substances; others navigated with caution, compliant to their raising. More or less. Blue jeans gave way to pierced ears, which caused Grandma Mattie to pray until the Christmas ham got cold that first year. But we were still family.

Grandma's funeral was well before the 2016 election, and—unbeknownst to us—the last Golden Day. We cried and laughed and sat at the wake eating Aunt Pat's Orange Delight Bundt Cream Cake and watching the children run. Wedding rings had created a whole new generation with different names but the same faces we remembered from childhood. We knew they would inherit our family creed and Aunt Pat's cake recipe along with those faces: glorify God; do right by your flesh and blood; avoid curling irons; cream the eggs and butter together before adding them to the dry ingredients.

By the time we gathered again to say goodbye to the first of the uncles, years had passed and we needed more than eggs to bind us. At the wake, the now-adult children of cousins, working their way through graduate school or a steel mill, offered jokes wrapped around baited hooks.

"That March of Women abomination in DC got more people walking than Michelle Obama ever did! Ha! Seriously though, he's gonna drain the swamp."

"You mean drain the Federal Reserves, don't you? Do you know how much golf he's played since becoming president? And his scores are worse than mine! Haha!"

The fundamentals felt the same—take care of your own, do what God says—but carefully manicured nails and up-swept curly hair dominated the room. The Aunts passed great-grandchildren back and forth and kept silence against their granddaughters in business suits. The granddaughters responded by twisting their wedding rings and sharing about the churches they had settled into back home—home being everything from Hugeopolis to Nowhereville along I-75. Churches where "family" meant ALL God's children, red and blue, black and white. They spoke of living wages at $15 per hour, single payer healthcare systems, and staying out of Walmart.

Two of the cousins, who now worked in what Tazewell had become, were refugees from Flint's bad water. The other two had given up trying to reclaim the old home stomping grounds in Detroit after they found that bullets from angry drug dealers would come calling, but the police would not. These couples grimaced and said they'd have been glad to have a Walmart near them, all that time they were trying to rebuild in a state ruined by entitlement. They narrated first-person experiences that proved God hated freeloaders. A family took care of its own. A real family, at least.

The Orange Delight cake stayed on its plate because half the room was on a plant-based diet after hearing a TED talk about the links between global warming and personal health, and the other half were diabetic from eating out in Hazard, Kentucky.

The Aunts could see what was happening, so they did what Appalachian Yankees do in times of crisis.

"Y'all quit that politics talk and get over here and finish up this ham. We're family," said Aunt Evelyn.

"It can be difficult to understand God's word in the context of today's challenges." Aunt Edna shoved paper plates of Orange Delight cake into our hands as she spoke. "But you can't argue with your mouths full. Eat."

Aunt Lelah looked sideways at Aunt Edna. "God's word never changes."

Aunt Edna blinked, fork halfway to her mouth. Her granddaughter Sally answered instead. "No, but life's circumstances do, and God gave us brains for a reason."

Uncle Ernie jabbed his plastic fork at Sally. "We must not question God's word. It tells us that earthly governments are ordained by God."

Cousin Alannis rolled her eyes and opened her mouth. Within ten minutes, people were leaving. I think it will be the last time I'll ever see some of them. We will tell ourselves that this is the way family works, breaking down into smaller units after the loss of Grandma Mattie. That time's inevitable march dictates The Aunts become matriarchs of their own tribes. We will not allow ourselves to believe that anything else happened here, this day we didn't know would not be golden with family and Bundt cake.

God love Cousin Alannis with her MBA and spiked heels. In her life, in the lives of her brothers and sisters, respect never became a word that shielded others from consequences. God bless Cousin Sally in her long denim skirt and sneakers, yards of poker-straight hair piled atop a head full of brains; she taught her nine children to question everything, just like she'd been doing since age three.

Did the women at wakes and weddings those hot summer days in 1860s Tazewell think similar things, adding their layer to the Apple Stack Cake built family by family, each contributing a piece to the whole? Did they watch the heat storms roll toward them from the edge of the valley, listen to trapped thunder beat itself to death against the mountain walls, and hear warnings of what was coming? When they prayed for rain, perhaps it was to cool the land and grow peace in their families, while brothers argued states' rights over picnic tables laden with food and cousins spit watermelon seeds at each other across the creek. Maybe they prayed for the safety of cousins gone to the North, whom they would never see again.

When did they know seeds would turn to bullets? When did they recognize that even families come apart at the seams so carefully sewn for generations by advice at the breakfast table, through careful introductions of cherished daughters to boys with no plans to move away, with recipes in scrawling script on scraps of paper stuck between college textbook pages as grandchildren head toward The City?

The Aunts looked defeated as they gathered up plates of uneaten Orange Delight from around the room. It is not an expression I am used to seeing on these faces my family has been sharing for so long.

Politics is one thing, family another. How much power does a president have to reach into the very hearts of people and turn watermelon seeds into bullets?

Scars
by Diane Wood

"It is in herself she will find her strength,
the strength she needs." —Tyler Knott Gregson

Dropping the phone onto the receiver, I stared mindlessly out the window beyond the infinite Tucson sky. A jet trail staggered north over the Davis-Monthan Air Force Base and across the coral horizon. In stark contrast, a fluorescent green hummingbird whirred upright, landing on the red plastic feeder outside the dusty kitchen window.

"God damn it, Mom," I muttered between gritted teeth to no one in particular.

My mother was still in Colorado where I'd left her when I moved to Tucson to start my business—a much-needed separation from her. But now her health was declining and, recently, she was not answering her phone when I called to check on her. She was beginning to scare me, on top of pissing me off. Not what I was thinking when I chose to put some mileage between the two of us. I hated that she was seemingly needing extra support now that I'd finally struck out on my own. Where in the freakin' hell had mother dearest been when I got sick and spent a week in the hospital a couple years ago? Did she even call me? No. Not until I got home. Then, when I was at home recovering for three months, and my car got totaled by a drunk driver at eight a.m. on my way to a dental appointment, would she let me borrow one of hers? Hell no. Did I owe her what she'd never given me?

I sat down at the kitchen table and had the thought that the time had come for me to contact Malaya, a woman I had met at a wedding reception a few months ago. Maybe she could help me see what was going on with Mom. I didn't know what else to do that could help me understand things on a different level. I needed spiritual guidance to figure out what my responsibility was.

I'd been packing things up after catering a wedding reception when this larger-than-life woman had filled the kitchen doorway.

She'd said, "I've been told to talk to you." The words flowed out in a low, smooth-as-caramel voice.

"Okay, but I'm busy at the moment." I was tired and really didn't feel like talking. "My business cards are over on that counter. If you'd like to call me tomorrow, we can talk then." I smiled at her, to be polite and professional.

"No, that won't work. You don't understand."

The pushy woman walked into the kitchen and stood too close for my comfort.

"Please listen. I have a message for you from someone who calls you Peanut."

The hair stood up on the back of my neck. I stopped what I was doing, pivoted, and stared up into her large, dark eyes.

Taking a few steps backward into my comfort zone, I asked, "What are you talking about?"

"We just need to talk." She never broke eye contact with me. That in itself unnerved me.

"I'll go say my goodbyes to the family and maybe we can talk outside for a few minutes." I swigged a few gulps from a half-empty, half-flat bottle of Freixenet Champagne, and belched unapologetically.

Some thirty minutes later, we sat in my packed station wagon and this stranger attempted to explain to me that she was a recently indoctrinated Shawoman (my title), and one of her abilities was working with the spirits on the other side to help people living on this earthly side. She'd been meditating one afternoon a few days ago when she'd heard a man's voice.

"It said, 'Tell Peanut I love her more than anything.' When I asked my guides for clarification, they showed me my nephew's wedding, and said that Peanut was the one in the chef's hat."

"Oh, well see; that's ridiculous. I've never in my life even wanted to wear a chef's hat. I think they're silly-looking." I gulped down a few more swigs of the room-temperature champagne I'd carried with me to the car.

"It's symbolic." Malaya answered. "Just pay attention."

"You know I believe in spirits and life after death and all that stuff, and Dad did call me Peanut, but what you're telling me is really way out there. Why would someone who died seventeen years ago suddenly want to make contact now?"

It was dark out, and that made the conversation and the setting—in a church parking lot, next to the church cemetery—a bit creepier. Goose bumps raised on my skin. The yellow glow from the lights made the guests leaving the wedding appear like shadows floating in the darkness. I wanted this conversation to be over with.

"I don't know, all I can say is, in my experience, it happens. There is no such thing as time, as we know it, on the other side. Those who have crossed over often have messages to deliver, and they need someone on this side to help deliver it. That's where I come in. I'm just a messenger."

Not really trusting her, but also wanting to, I asked if she could connect with my dad right there as we sat in my car behind Holy Cross Catholic Church. Malaya said she couldn't offer me a guarantee but was willing to give it a try.

"You don't always know for sure who's going to show up. Okay? Now I'm going to close my eyes and see if he comes through."

Exhausted, I was impatient with this strange person, more than I would normally be with someone I didn't know. Maybe I was feeling a tad bit tipsy from the warm champagne. For all I knew this woman could be a crazy-ass, wedding crasher. I finished off the last two swigs of champagne and unconsciously scraped off strips of the damp label with my thumbnail. I rolled them up and pushed the little, wet wads into the empty bottle. Even though I was intrigued by this encounter, I was about to start the car and kick the weirdo out.

"Okay—yes, I'll tell her. I said I. Will. Tell. Her!"

"Is that my dad? You got him? Let me talk to him," I pleaded, grabbing her arm.

"No. Oh! No. Don't talk," Malaya sighed. "Ugh—he's gone. I forgot to tell you to wait until I opened my eyes. It breaks my energetic connection. I need more practice at this. I haven't been doing this all that long," she confessed.

"So you think you saw my father? What did he say? What'd he look like?"

"I didn't see him, I heard him. He was pretty adamant for some reason. He said, 'Tell Peanut how much I love her and to please keep an eye on Janie.'"

I opened my eyes wide. Janie was my Mom. This woman couldn't know that. I was becoming convinced she was the real deal. Suddenly my heart sank that Mom was the topic. "That's it? What does he mean specifically?" I'd heard of things like this happening, but, yikes!

"Then he said, 'Tell Peanut whenever she feels that little tickle on the scar on her forehead, it's me reminding her that I'm around. She doesn't have to feel alone—ever." Then she handed me her card, got out of my car, and wished me well.

Apparently, before her spiritual awakening, Malaya had been a high school science teacher, until she was overwhelmed by a spiritual calling. After a lot of woo-woo training with the Huichol Indians in Mexico, she became a certified Shawoman. Word of her expertise spread like heat waves in the new-agey Tucson underground. With her large, formidable, dark-skinned body and wild, ebony hair, she could have been a Pacific Islander, or Native American, or Hispanic. Not that it mattered. My mind flipped back to when Dee Brown's *Bury My Heart at Wounded Knee* had first been published in 1970, and it suddenly became very cool to mention there was Native blood running through your veins. The tribe of origin didn't even matter at that time, nor did the percentage of blood.

I called Malaya to explain what was going on with my mother's health. It felt like a mystery, a very scary mystery. I didn't want to give Malaya too much information; but enough to let her weave her magic, if she could. We decided to meet at her house an hour after our call.

My car drove pretty much on autopilot during the half-hour trek into the desert southwest of Tucson. No matter where I looked, all I saw was beige on the ground around me and blue above. The view was the same thing pretty much every single, solitary, boring-weather day.

I made a left onto So. Camino Poton El Dorado. This up-scale area was not the type of community where I'd imagined a Shawoman living and practicing. If landscaped lawns had been practical in the desert, this was exactly the kind of place where the covenants would keep residents from mowing them on Sundays.

It was so bright that, even wearing sunglasses, I needed to squint to read the house numbers. The numbers were going up—the direction I needed to go. Her house was at the apex of the cul-de-sac with nothing behind it except the wide, open desert. I parked in the driveway and walked up the slab stone steps to a huge, hammered copper, double door. As I lifted the heavy, crescent moon knocker, the door opened.

"Welcome." An ebullient Malaya wrapped her ample arms around me drawing me into her space. She wasn't as intimidating in the daylight. Malaya's touch quelled some of my anxiety, but my goose bumps belied the fact that the outside temperature was a hundred and twelve degrees, even in the semi-shade of the old saguaros.

"Follow me." Malaya sashayed down the hallway.

In the coolness of the tiled entryway, faintly scented with lavender, my anxiety moved down another notch. Massive, exotic houseplants flanked the north wall behind ice green, wicker furniture. I followed Malaya into the sunroom behind the kitchen. A bright green, feathered bird, with a big round, red belly sat on a perch in a partially sunlit corner and eyed me curiously.

"His name is Chimi," Malaya explained. "He's a Quetzel. A gift from the Huichol Indians in Mexico after my final mara'akame, or Shawoman initiation ceremony."

We sat down across from each other in Malaya's ceremony room at an octagonal wooden table. The top was inlaid with amethyst, silver, and onyx tiles set into the shape of what looked like a Mayan calendar. I'd once seen a picture of something similar in a *National Geographic* magazine. It symbolized the sun. The inlaid figures were deities, hieroglyphs, and feathered serpents representing the Earth's journey around the sun.

Malaya spoke first. "Since we first talked, I've been picturing your mother as somewhat of a girl-child playing the role of femme fatale."

I responded, "She's emotionally immature and very insecure. But a femme fatale?"

Malaya continued, "What I experience in my body, when I focus on her in my mind, is a tingling numbness. My hands sense heat, like hot pads." She stretched her arms across the table, palms up.

"Feel."

I held my hands a couple inches above her long, light-colored palms. It felt as if I were holding them over a smoldering campfire.

"What's that mean?" I asked, pulling my hands back.

"Give me a minute." Malaya closed her eyes inhaling and exhaling slowly. "Mmm, uh-huh." She repeated it a few times. I now knew not to interrupt her until she opened her eyes.

While I waited for her, I thought of how once when I was around five years old, I split my head open when I slipped and fell on the gravel street in front of our house playing Red Rover with a few of the neighborhood kids. It is such a vivid memory. I walked to my house holding my forehead over my palm and watching the deep, red blood drip, drip, drip methodically and then roll through my fingers onto the pavement in a small red splat. Dad called the hospital, and ironically got Mom, who was a switchboard operator, to put the call through. She was concerned but wasn't able to leave work.

He rushed me to the hospital, holding a towel on my head with one hand and driving with the other, comforting me over and over again. "Don't worry, Peanut, I'm here. Everything's going to be alright," my dad had repeated to me.

While Malaya's eyes remained closed so she could give me a message about my mother, I thought more about Dad. I remember feeling safe. I remember knowing that my dad would take care of me. I didn't notice Mom's absence during that hospital visit, didn't feel there was anything missing. And of course, I didn't know at that time my father would be present with me in a way that my mother wasn't as I grew up, in a way that she never would be able to be.

Now, sitting across from Malaya in her ceremony room, my skepticism was replaced by my need to understand more about my mother and my own challenges as a result of her untold story.

Malaya began to speak slowly now. "Your mother's very tired. In her deep subconscious she's trying to decide if it's time for her to go, or if she needs to stay to complete more lessons in this lifetime before she crosses over. She's experiencing loneliness on so many levels. In one sense, her life is everything she's ever fantasized about—the money, the security, her ability to travel, her freedom to paint, and the prestige of the man she's married to. But like most human beings, her true longings run deep beneath the surface. When she's alone with just herself, she finds only the animal world to comfort her. She and her dogs and cats understand each other."

My heart felt Malaya's words. I began to believe Malaya was the real deal. She was able to connect with the unseen world on the other side. This was exactly what I needed—help on a spiritual level. Hot tears trickled down my face. I needed all of what she was telling me to be the truth because I carried so much daughter guilt, always feeling like I should be doing more for Mom's well-being while also wishing I could break away from her neediness and live my own life. I trusted Malaya's message was the truth.

She spoke again now. "Listen. Every miniscule choice we make has an effect on something or someone. It especially impacts our own journey; every thought, every movement. The Universe is energy; we are all energy and all that energy is continuously ebbing and flowing according to each thought and each action one makes. It's cliché, but thoughts are things. You decide 'yes' and you end up going right; decide 'no' and end up going left, hypothetically speaking."

"I never seem to make the right choices with regard to my mother, Malaya. I need you to tell me what to do. Should I go back to Colorado and be the dutiful daughter, as always, or can I continue to build a new life here in Tucson?"

"Your guides are always with you if you need them. You just need to be open to them. I can only help you by telling you the truth I see," Malaya said. "Decisions are always up to the individual. Everything matters," Malaya went on. "Your choices will affect other's choices, and theirs will affect yours and others and so on. Right here, right now, this is *your* personal journey. At the same time, your mother is on her personal journey. On the physical level every human being is on their own personal journey, whether we're aware of it or not. Both you and your mother have choices you need to make according to agreements you made before you were born into this life."

What in the world was I supposed to do with this information? Should I go back and take care of Mom? She's the reason I moved out here. I was so tired of being the grown-up in our relationship.

"Well, that doesn't help me decide if I should drop my life and go back to Colorado."

"I'm with you on this journey of yours, as are your guides. Just remember you're never alone."

Small consolation, but I took it. I would have some big decisions to make. For the first time in my life, I would have support from a woman of wisdom.

ACKNOWLEDGMENTS

We know it takes a village (more like a midsized city) to bring a book into the world. First, we want to thank our families and partners for their support. Significant resources and time have gone into writing these stories. And everyone inside a household has to participate in holding space for a writer. Thank you for being committed to our dreams.

Thank you also to the coaches in The Narrative Project. Anni, Colleen, Nancy, Rebecca, and Wendy are the rock stars who hold our writers accountable, inspire them to write, and say, "You can do it" when their confidence flags.

Gratitude to the awesome staff at Third Place Books at Ravenna in Seattle, who have ALL cheered us on and will continue to do so once the pandemic is over and we are allowed to gather again for open mic. We love you and miss you. Also, deep gratitude to Village Books in Bellingham, Washington, for being constantly in our corner. In Bellingham as well, the Red Wheelbarrow Writers are both inspiration and example to our community. We so appreciate cross-pollinating with you.

Finally, our publisher, Sidekick Press is headed up by one of our own, Lisa Dailey. We are grateful for you and we bow to you, Lisa.

August Cabrera

August, a surviving military spouse, recently moved to North Carolina with her two boys and their neurotic Sheltie. Currently working on her first book about her relationship with her husband (before and after his death), she is enjoying the challenge and adventure of finally following her dream of being a writer when she grows up.

Nancy Canyon

Nancy Canyon is the author of *Saltwater*, a book of poetry, and a novel, *Celia's Heaven*, which is the winner of Chanticleer Review's Cygnus Award for Paranormal Fiction. With an MFA in Creative Writing from Pacific Lutheran University, Nancy coaches for The Narrative Project and teaches for Chuckanut Writers. She lives with her husband in Bellingham, Washington. *A Terrible Storm* is an excerpt from Nancy Canyon's forthcoming memoir, "Struck."

Al Clover

At the age of six, Al Clover stood in front of the grocery store spin rack, and the MAD Magazine—with the iconic "What, Me Worry?" cover—enticed him to spend his weekly allowance. Somehow that led him to writing his first book, "The Comic Book Detective." That's his story and he's sticking to it. albclover.com

Lisa Dailey

Lisa Dailey is an avid traveler and writer. *Losing Control* is an excerpt from her forthcoming memoir, "Square Up", detailing the adventures and misadventures of a seven-month trip around the world as well as her own personal journey through grief. Through her publishing and web design companies, Lisa helps authors with a wide range of technical and publishing needs. sidekickpress.com

Seán Dwyer

Seán Dwyer teaches Spanish at Western Washington University and has published a memoir, *A Quest for Tears: Surviving Traumatic Brain Injury*, as well as a number of short stories. An advocate for emerging writers, he hosts open mics at a local bookstore. A native of Gary, Indiana, Seán now resides in Bellingham, Washington, with his wife, Maureen, his hairless cat, Luna, and his Angora goat, Bob. *Unbearably Beautiful* is an excerpt from Seán's forthcoming novel, "Chocolates on My Pillow."

Colleen Haggerty

Colleen Haggerty is a writer of memoir and personal essay who has been published in various anthologies. Her memoir, *A Leg to Stand On*, a finalist for the National Indie Excellence Awards, recounts her journey into motherhood as an amputee. An inspirational speaker and coach, Colleen gave a TEDx talk, "Forgiving the Unforgivable." Colleen is a writing coach for The Narrative Project.

Alyson Indrunas

Alyson Indrunas has published essays in *The Listening Eye*, *The Evansville Review*, *Big Muddy: A Journal of the Mississippi River Valley*, *Clickers in the Classroom*, and *Adventures Northwest*. *The Kind of People Who Leave Dirt on the Floor* is an excerpt from her memoir-in-process, "What the Shoulders Can Bear." She lives in Bellingham, Washington, and blogs at spokeandhub.blog.

Anneliese Kamola

Anneliese Kamola is an author, developmental editor, and Narrative Project coach living in Bellingham, Washington. Her memoir is forthcoming in 2021. She is co-editor of TNP's *True Stories: Vols. II and III*. Anneliese writes on themes of the body, family history, and what makes us human. Check out her blog at anneliesekamola.com/blog.

Christina Kemp

Christina Kemp has been a lover of writing since her early years and continues her dedication to the written word in her home in the Pacific Northwest. She is a psychology professor, writer, counselor, and re-emerging dancer living on Bainbridge Island.

Rebecca Mabanglo-Mayor

Rebecca Mabanglo-Mayor's non-fiction, poetry, and short fiction have appeared in print and online in several journals and anthologies. She is also the co-editor of *True Stories: The Narrative Project Vols. I-III*, and her poetry and essays have been collected in *Dancing Between Bamboo Poles*.

Judith Mayotte

In the late 1980s, Judith Mayotte received the MacArthur Foundation grant to write her book, *Disposable People?: The Plight of Refugees*. Today, she continues to speak on behalf of millions displaced by extreme weather events in a changing climate and millions more who will experience climate change displacement. Judith lives in Seattle, Washington.

G. Annie Ormsby

Annie Ormsby is a native of the Northwest who spends most of her time exploring the natural world and other tender and wild places while loving and learning from her two children and husband. A bodyworker for humans and horses, she forever marvels at the beauty and power of intent and connection.

Cami Ostman

Cami Ostman, founder of The Narrative Project, has published a memoir, *Second Wind: One Woman's Midlife Quest to Run Seven Marathons on Seven Continents*, and has co-edited several anthologies, including *Beyond Belief: The Secret Lives of Women in Extreme Religions* and *True Stories, Vols. I-III*. She has been profiled in *Fitness Magazine* and her books have been reviewed in *O Magazine*, *The Atlantic*, and *The Washington Post*.

Aaron C Palmer

Aaron C Palmer writes edgy, cross-genre long- and short-form fiction and screenplays filled with gripping scenes and lively characters. He finds inspiration from family and hiking the rugged Pacific Northwest trails with his squirrel-crazy pup. *Quest of the Buckwheaters* is an excerpt from Aaron's forthcoming novel, "Frontier Sugar." Published by Tolosa Press, Sidekick Press, and various underground media. ac-palmer.com

Kathy Wagner

Kathy Wagner is a Canadian addictions support advocate who writes about family, grief, hope, addiction, recovery, and finding joy. She's honed her writing skills through The Narrative Project and the Banff Writers Retreat, and has multiple pieces published in *The Globe and Mail*. You can read more from Kathy at kwagnerwrites.com or follow her on Instagram @kwagner_writes.

M. F. Webb

M. F. Webb is a former Texan and current resident of Washington State, a writer of poetry, fiction, and now collage memoir. Her poetry has appeared in *Spectral Realms* and her fiction has been published in *Latchkey Tales*. *Desert Daughter* is an excerpt from her work in progress, "All These Things Are True."

Wendy Welch

Wendy Welch has a doctorate in ethnography and is the author of five books, including *The Little Bookstore of Big Stone Gap*. She teaches cultural competency to medical professionals and lives in rural Virginia with her husband, rescue dogs and cats, two pet chickens, and a weedy garden.

Diane Wood

Diane Wood wrote in her high school yearbook, "Now I'm going out into the world and have all kinds of exciting experiences. When I'm old I shall write about them." She had the experiences and is now writing about them. Wood's memoir, "Vital Signs: A Mother, A Daughter, and Deathbed Secrets," is her favorite. *Scars* is an excerpt from Diane Wood's forthcoming memoir, "Vital Signs: A Mother, A Daughter, and Deathbed Secrets"